1 MONTH OF
FREE
READING

at

www.ForgottenBooks.com

By purchasing this book you are eligible for one month membership to ForgottenBooks.com, giving you unlimited access to our entire collection of over 700,000 titles via our web site and mobile apps.

To claim your free month visit:

www.forgottenbooks.com/free776529

ISBN 978-0-483-27843-1
PIBN 10776529

This book is a reproduction of an important historical work. Forgotten Books uses
state-of-the-art technology to digitally reconstruct the work, preserving the original format
whilst repairing imperfections present in the aged copy. In rare cases, an imperfection in
the original, such as a blemish or missing page, may be replicated in our edition. We do,
however, repair the vast majority of imperfections successfully; any imperfections that
remain are intentionally left to preserve the state of such historical works.

SAKUNTALA

OR

THE LOST RING.

SAKUNTALA

OR

THE LOST RING.

SAKUNTALA, A PLAY IN FIVE ACTS, BY J. G. JENNINGS, *Allahabad, Indian Press*, 1902 : 210 *pages, paper covers,* 6s. ; *cloth, gilt tops,* 7s. 6d. (*200 copies only*).

BY THE SAME WRITER :

MASQUE OF THE THREE LOVES, *Allahabad, Indian Press,* 1902 : 165 *pages, cloth, gilt tops,* 6s. (*200 copies only*).

QUATRAINS, *Allahabad, Indian Press,* 1901 : 83 *pages, cloth, gilt taps,* 3s. 6d. (*200 copies only*).

(VERSES) FROM AN INDIAN COLLEGE, *London, Kegan Paul, Trench, Trubner and Co., Ltd.,* 1898 : 119 *pages, cloth, gilt tops,* 3s. 6d. net.

ṢAKUNTALA

A PLAY IN FIVE ACTS

BY

J. G. JENNINGS

——:o:——

ALLAHABAD:
INDIAN PRESS,
1902.

Printed at the INDIAN PRESS, Allahabad.

INTRODUCTORY NOTE.

The following play is based upon the Indian drama *Sakuntala, or The Lost Ring*, by the famous Sanskrit poet Kalidasa. I am especially indebted to Sir Monier Monier-Williams' translation. The original story has been treated with great freedom.

J. G. J.

DRAMATIS PERSONÆ.

DUSHYANTA, *the young King of Hastinapur.*

MADHAVYA, *cousin of* DUSHYANTA.

BHARATA, *the little son of* DUSHYANTA *and* SAKUNTALA.

KANWA, *prior of a monastery, and foster-father of* SAKUNTALA.

DURVASAS, *an ascetic.*

SOMARATA, *household priest to the King.*

SAKUNTALA, *a princess, foster-daughter of* KANWA.

PRIYAMVADA ⎫
⎬ *companions of* SAKUNTALA.
ANASUYA ⎭

GAUTAMI, *prioress of a monastery.*

Monks, Pupils, Fishermen, Chamberlain, Courtiers, Officers, Page, Servants, Nuns, Maidens of the Palace, Huntsman, Nurse, Attendant, and others.

NOTE :

The vowels of Indian names are pronounced as in the Latin languages. An accent on any syllable of an Indian name in the following pages indicates stress, not quantity.

SAKUNTALA, OR THE LOST RING.

A PLAY IN FIVE ACTS.

ACT I, Scene i.

SCENE: *the outskirts of a forest, in the neighbourhood of a monastery: round one of the trees in the foreground (left) is a low platform of earth, and upon it a small shrine and growing plants; creepers overgrow the neighbouring trees. In the background a forest is seen curving from the East (left) to the North and West below the first spurs of the Himalayas: at some distance on the Western side (right) is seen the River Málini, which flows in a slow broad stream among many sandbanks; and spreading from the river to the borders of the forest is a wide meadow-like expanse.* TIME: *noon.*

[TWO MONKS *are discovered.*

1ST MONK (*stopping*).

Can you not hear unwonted sounds in the air?

Hark ! for they rise again—and yet again—
Far, faint, and rare.

2ND MONK (*listening*).

         Ay, in this quiet region
The voice of man sounds rarely with such clamour.
The woods beyond the river are alive
With stirring men. See there, the flash of steel !
Lo ! near and far !—spearheads belike, that shoot
Their gleams beyond the puny range of sound.

1ST MONK.

What is it, brother ? Cometh further woe
To pack its load on what already galls us ?
I fear—

2ND MONK.

    See, see, the jewelled light of the steel,
How like a coronet woven in dark hair
It flashes through our Málini's dusk woods !
And one gem blazes ever before the crown,
A kingdom's ransom. 'Tis the king ! the king!
Now all are out: the trees extinguish all,

And westward streams the hunt away.—Yea, brother,
It is none other than the king our lord.
A mighty hunter is the youth our king.

1st MONK.

Nay, nay! Let him then hunt elsewhere! We want
No blood and riot in these solemn lands.

2nd MONK.

His is a high and strenuous spirit, brother;
Fierce blood that springs upon each task and grips,
Nor looses hold till it be overthrown—
Whether state's work or pleasure be his quarry.
It is a fair young spirit. Tenderness
Will come in time, with his advancing years.

       [*The* Two Monks *go out (left).*

     A voice (*heard calling from some distance*).
Sakúntala! Sakúntala!

       [*Enter* Sakuntala *and* Anasuya
         (*centre*), *carrying water-jars.*

ANASUYA.

How far
She strays behind !

SAKUNTALA (*turning and gazing back*).
What can have kept her ? Call !

VOICE (*heard calling*).
Oh ! Anasúya !

ANASUYA (*calls*).
Oh ! Priyamváda ! Come,
Sweet laggard, come ! (*To* SAKUNTALA:) Well, let us
rid ourselves
Of these our burdens. (*As they set down their jars:*)

There !—The heated noon
Breaks in a-glow ev'n on these forest bowers,
Where his cold love lies dreaming deep in shade.

SAKUNTALA.

Oh, that she wake and with her chilly eyes
Drive him in scorn back to the noisy world !

ANASUYA.

Yea ! Haply, though, the wooing sun will laugh,
And clasp her close, and kiss the cold eyes warm.

Such things have been.

> [PRIYAMVADA *enters (centre), also bearing a*
> *water-jar.*

SAKUNTALA.

Well, laggard, hast thou come?

PRIYAMVADA (*setting down her jar*).

Oh, the weight of it!   And then a tiresome thorn
Dragged at my skirt: I scarce could get it free.
But what things "have been," Anasúya, pray?

ANASUYA.

Love hath been, Priyamváda.

PRIYAMVADA.

                    Love, oh, love!
Not in these sacred groves, thou daring spirit!
Here nothing loves—save birds, and beasts, and flowers,
The earth, the sky, the sun, the gushing rain,
The—all things, O Sakúntala, belovèd,
Excepting man and maiden, by our rules,

ANASUYA.

Yet let them come, the still unknown, to woo!

Are we not free to love ? Our pupil age
Is over.

PRIYAMVADA.

Well, let them come !

SAKUNTALA.

      Set we to work
Upon the task of love nearest our hands,
To fill the parching channels round our trees,
That these dear plants may drink. For Heaven has
 made

The flowers and us akin. These are our sisters,
Whom passion never soils, that never stray,
Whose love estrangement never rends asunder.
God is in all, all lives are God's alone,
Whose sole life peopled all his worlds with lives;
And some have soared, and some have climbed with
 pain

Partly the distance back to Heaven's fond heart,
And some have strayed, and lie apart ; and some,
Like these fair flowers, have never left God's bosom.

> [*All three take up their jars and begin
> to water the flowers and creepers.*

PRIYAMVADA (*pausing*).

Do you not hear some far, unwonted sound ?
Hark !   It is louder now.   (*As all pause :*) 'Tis blown
  this way.

> [*She runs towards the edge of
> the forest (right) and gazes.*

Oh, oh ! (*wringing her hands*).

SAKUNTALA.

What do you see ?   Why do you cry ?

> [*She and* ANASUYA *follow quickly.*

Oh, shame ! shame ! shame !   To chase our gentle
  deer !
Sweet creatures that have found all men their friends,
And now in all will see but enemies—
How should their simple hearts know friend and
  foe !

To break such love !
2

ANASUYA.

Oh, evil deed !

PRIYAMVADA.

He shall

Not kill it ! Escape, escape ! Leap, leap !

ANASUYA.

'Tis free !

SAKUNTALA.

Blessings upon our wood that guards its child !

ANASUYA.

See, he dismounts. I think the hunter paused :
He might have struck, but spared.

PRIYAMVADA.

Then, bless him too !

See, he salutes the lower shrine. Dost see ?
He is pious then, as well as merciful.
A great chief in the land too. Lo, what steeds !
The gilded car ! The goodly charioteer !
He hands him now what golden ornaments,

Stipped from what neck, what arms! And now his bow,

Fit for a hero-king! He will not come

Into these holy groves adorned and armed.

Oh, splendid youth, jewelled with modesty!

SAKUNTALA.

He comes this way. Let us begone!

PRIYAMVADA.

Alack!

ANASUYA.

He must have heard your soul's apostrophe.

PRIYAMVADA.

Then flee, then flee! (*As they run* :) But not too far, beseech you.

> [*They run off (centre) leaving their water-jars. As they disappear,* KING DUSHYANTA *enters (right).*
>
> KING (*looking back*).

(*Calling* :) Here I will wait. Bid all assemble hither.

> [*He looks round.*

(*To self* :) Yea, it is holy ground : I well withheld
The fatal shaft.   The shrine below forewarned.
The shrine here too; grain for the nesting birds ;
These plants ; and all things set in kindly order !
Ah, here are water-jars—full too !   (*Laughing* :) In-
   truder !
Thou hast disturbed the timid gardeners.
Fie on my violence, who by title am
Guardian of all things holy !

        [*Enter the* Two Monks *hastily* (*left*).

        Whom have we here ?—

Greeting, O fathers !

        Monks (*raising their hands*).

        Heaven's blessing be upon thee,

Illustrious son !

        [*As they begin their benediction,
        the* King *sinks upon one knee.*

        King.

        And upon ye, my fathers

Your benedictions fall on grateful soil,
That shall bring forth to you an hundredfold,
Your own good grain up-sprung.

1st MONK.

O king, be thine
The tender joy of children, for no other
Of earthly joys burns with such purging fire
Within the hearts of the mighty!

2nd MONK.

Yea, be thine
A son, to light his heart under thy heart,
That he may flare a great course after thee
Over an arc that little men may know
But by the flaming of your starry spirits!

KING (*rising*).

I am but young, and all untried, my fathers:
Let your prayers keep me, lest I stumble and fall!

2nd MONK.

As we two walked, sire, yonder slowly homeward,

[*He points to front.*

Through the sparse trees that fringe our sacred
    groves,
Conversing of the things that were, and are,
And that shall be, we marked your fiery course
—With panting hearts as pants the laboured prey.
Nigh and more nigh, the straining deer before,
The bow upraised, the shaft poised for the wing !
Then sudden change (belike our prayers had power) :
Bow down, the shaft a-droop, the charioteer
With rooted feet and rigid arm and rein,
And horses carven before the car as stone !
So sped we back, through shortest woodland paths,
To bid glad welcome to the approaching guest.
Thrice welcome, king, and doubly thrice be welcome ;
Not only for thy being stranger here,
But for thy youth and graciousness, my king !
Ill is the doom of them that fail to greet
The wandering stranger with all needful aid ;
Who comes protected by Heaven's shadowing hand,
Through burning day, through slow dew-dropping
    night ;
Most ill the doom of them that fail and are
Themselves but mendicants among the folk,

Beggars of alms, that they may live with God
All day and every day till true Day come!
But not for this alone, fair king, be welcome;
Be welcome equally for thou art thou!

KING.

My heart can bear its load of gratitude,
Dear father, easier than tell of it.

1ST MONK.

Then shalt thou, sire, mind thee in times to come
Our needs are sore; whose willing power of good
Is yoked with a dull jade, that holds it back;
Galled, halt, and curst—men call it poverty.

KING (*laughing*).

Nay, father, trust me! I will feed thy jade
With the best oats I know for such as he
—The good fat land itself—at morrow's dawn,
So you will house me for the night-time here.
This night your boundaries shall lie in travail,
And with the morning shall give birth to fields.
Scribes are at hand, to play the busy midwife.
It is my fancy, sirs, ev'n in the chase,

Mid shifting camps and ever-changing scenes,
To hold such threads of governance as I may,
And still to weave the pattern of my rule.
They come behind, by slow laborious roads,
Bringing the substance that I spin withal;
And couriers ever flitting to and fro
Are still the busy shuttles of my loom.
Blame their delay, dear father, if in aught
I fail to make my promise good at dawn,

1ST MONK.

All blessings in my power, O king, had flown
From out my soul up to the ultimate heavens,
And bowed and pleaded, and assurance heard,
In thy loved cause, before thy promise given;
And I stand beggared here of all but thanks.

2ND MONK.

Come, sire ! Your feet being honour where they rest :
We are impatient till they rest with us.
Our prior is gone from home—he has been gone
These many days; and many more may plunge
Into the caldron of the western sea

Where still he watches, ere he shall return.

His wisdom will be lacking in our aid,

Yet shall our zeal labour to make amends.

Come, sire !

KING.

Nay, father, pardon me awhile.

I needs must tarry till my folk appear.

1ST MONK.

Beseech you, sire, approach !   There shall be sent

A trusty brother that shall guide all on.

2ND MONK.

I will myself return.

KING.

Nay, father, be

This fresh boon mine—that I may pause behind you.

I am o'er-scrupulous perchance in word

—Perhaps (who knows ?) more clean without than in—

Yet since I bade him say I would be here,

Here I must be—and here I best can rule

The roughened ways of my good hunting train.

Yet let me come a few steps on your way.

2ND MONK.

So be it then ; and we will haste before
To spread the news and speed your welcoming.
The path is narrow at first, but turns aside
Soon in a wide-lain avenue of trees
That will not fail you.

KING.

Let me come so far.

[KING *and* MONKS *go out (left).*

PRIYAMVADA *and* ANASUYA
enter (centre) peeping ; SA-
KUNTALA *follows slowly.*

PRIYAMVADA.

He is gone.

ANASUYA.

Where ?

PRIYAMVADA.

Yonder. Do you see him ? Come !

[*She beckons to* SAKUNTALA.

SAKUNTALA.

I will not come.

PRIYAMVADA.

         So did you say before
—And yet have come.

SAKUNTALA.

      Well, I will come no further.

PRIYAMVADA.

—Than here where he returns. O darling, darling!
O simple fowler, and most lovely girl!
Thou hast no need to hide thy snares from me.

SAKUNTALA.

Nay, that is nonsense. That is most unfair.
Thou hast the hardest little heart in all
The world.

PRIYAMVADA (*laughing*).

And who, love, has the softest then?

SAKUNTALA (*turning away*).

Ah, Anasúya, to be sure.

PRIYAMVADA.

         Ha, ha!

Ha, ha!

ANASUYA (*to* SAKUNTALA).

For thee ! Thou know'st I have for thee.

> [*They move towards their water-jars.*
> SAKUNTALA *stoops to lift a jar,*
> *and in doing so places one hand*
> *against a tree.*

PRIYAMVADA.

O Anasúya, quick ! Look up and see
How like Sakúntala to yon fair plant,
Our tender jasmine, Moonlight of the Grove,
Clasping the mango-tree !

ANASUYA.

The moon-pale bride
That hides her face from love, who still looks down.

PRIYAMVADA.

Oh, look thou up, most beautiful of flowers !

> [SAKUNTALA *turns away; the*
> *others whisper and laugh. They*
> *water the plants.*

PRIYAMVADA.

Ah, Anasúya, would I were a saint!
Then would my prayers be heard, for saintly hearts
Dwell ever with heaven ; or, if to earth they come,
Swiftly to heaven return.

ANASUYA.

And since our souls
Are heavenly still, their burning prayers can weld
Us, here, to heaven again.   So we receive
New touch with the Divine beyond the worlds,
Through the saints' prayers.

SAKUNTALA.

Yea, and 'tis even so
When the saints pray us harm : they cleanse by pain.

PRIYAMVADA.

From me no harm.   But if I were a saint—

ANASUYA.

Ha, ha, ha, ha!

PRIYAMVADA.

Now, is not that provoking?
And why not, pray?

ANASUYA.

Thou art too sweetly mortal.

PRIYAMVADA.

Well, if I were not so, then I should pray
—For you, more reverence both to saints and me
—And for Sakúntala—what thinks't thou, dear?
A mate like one whom we have seen to-day?

[*The* KING *enters unseen (left) and hides.*

SAKUNTALA.

Take up thy task, thou silly maid.

PRIYAMVADA.

                     Thou 'dst think
I'd wished her ill.   Art thou not fair?

SAKUNTALA.

                        Oh, go!
Well art thou called the Flatterer—Priyamváda.

PRIYAMVADA.

I flatter where I love.

SAKUNTALA.

Say, where thou 'rt loved :
Thou canst not choose but flatter—everywhere.

[*They embrace.*

KING (*to self*).

The timid gardeners ! Maids, as I thought—
But fair passing all thought ! Hush ! lest they fly !...
Her humble garb makes her but seem the fairer,
Like to the moon, part-clad in shredded storm.
—Shame on me, shame ! Here do I lurk and spy,
Like some vile thief, upon maids' privacy,
Gaze on their hearts unzoned and unaware ?
Yet, should they flee ! I must go softly to it.

SAKUNTALA.

O Anasúya, a bee ! I wet him through,
And he is after me.

ANASUYA (*helping*).

Begone !

PRIYAMVADA.

Begone !

SAKUNTALA.

Ah, thou malicious little thing! Oh, help!

PRIYAMVADA.

Oh for a man to hide behind ! Help, help !
O king Dushyánta, guardian of our groves,
Send thou a knight to succour our distress !

> [*The* KING *laughingly ad-*
> *vances. The three girls*
> *stand together, startled*
> *and embarrassed.*

KING.

What caitiff dares to harm these lovely maids ?
The fiery tiger or the ravening boar
Would stand disarmed to gaze on such as these,
Fawning to be caressed by beauty's hands.
What, is a man, then, sentient less than beasts
To maiden loveliness ! Where doth he hide
His coward shame, that I may vengeance wreak ?

PRIYAMVADA (*smiling*).

Oh no, great sir, for vengeance is not known

Within these groves.

KING.

Most holy maids, whose souls
Are ev'n as lovely as their bodily features !

PRIYAMVADA.

Besides, sir, he is flown.

KING.

I will pursue.
Ah, should a cruel foe, at lurk, lie hid,
A spy upon your innocent steps, O maids,
None may be by to save; these fair devotions,
To which your maiden lives are dedicate,
Be trampled under foot in terror and noise.

PRIYAMVADA (*laughing*).

But he is flown with wings.

KING.

Ah, ladies, I
Am merely human: I but fight on earth.

3

SAKUNTALA.

Ye fight not here, kind sir : here is no evil,
Although the show of it has given high proof
Of your attempered chivalry to aid
Weakness distressed.   Be welcome here, O friend !
O guest ! shaft from the bow of heaven, God-sped !
Welcome, as angel and as stranger here
Are ever !

KING.

       The saints hear all prayers that thou
Put'st up to them ! (*To self :*) O queenly maid ! Be still,
My heart, lest she should speak from heaven again !

SAKUNTALA.

Do thou, my Anasuya, haste before.
Swiftly thou'lt tell them—Lo ! our guest is come.
(*To* KING :) My foster-father, Kanwa, is away ;
Yet, though 'tis priorless, our convent still
Shall fail not in right hospitality.—
Speed, love, along !—(*To* KING :) Or, come you with
    us, sir !

KING.

Nay, gentle maids, all guest-rites that are due
Your monks have paid. Yet take you thanks in turn.
Still must I tarry here, till my wild folk
Slowly arrive.

SAKUNTALA.

Rest then with us beneath
These hospitable shadows till they come.

[*All sit down.*

KING.

Ah, I would gladly pause the whole day long,
And aid you in your happy labours here ;
Work in your garden, ever fetch and carry,
Hew wood, draw water, help as dull strength can,
Your wits still leading where the strength should go.

[*Hunting bugles heard faintly.*

But yonder sound the bugles from the forest,
And hither troops my over-hasting train
Headlong across the lea. (*Rising :*) Go then, sweet maids !
For these are rough-hewn men, full of wild jests
At all that is too fair and pure for laughter.
Yet do not hide. There shall be stern control—

I vouch it it on my life.   Awhile adieu !

> ⌊*He advances (right), but before leaving turns and gazes.*

MAIDENS.

Adieu !

KING *(to self)*.

The prior's foster-daughter ? Who is the maid ?

> [*He goes out. The girls gaze meaningly at* SAKUNTALA.

ANASUYA.

O Sakúntala !

PRIYAMVADA.

O belovèd !

SAKUNTALA *(after a pause, dreamily)*.

Well ?

PRIYAMVADA.

Come !

> [*They lead her away (left). As they go out the* KING's *retinue is heard approaching.*

CURTAIN.

ACT I, Scene ii.

Scene: *the outskirts of a forest, as before.* Time:
afternoon, drawing towards evening.

> [*The* King *and* Madhavya *are*
> *discovered, the former pacing*
> *to and fro, the latter reclining*
> *whilst he watches the other.*
> *The* King *pauses and flings*
> *himself down, hiding his face*
> *with a passionate movement.*

MADHAVYA.

This much is plain—thou art the devotee.
But whether it be shrine of saint or beauty
Thou dost thy worship at, I see not clearly,

KING.

Ah, Mádhavya! (*Checks himself.*)

MADHAVYA.

Well?

KING (*averting his face*).

Nothing.

MADHAVYA.

Pregnant word!

Eloquent silence! To my gazing mind
The picture rises slow—a rustic maiden,
Fresh as the milk that bubbles in her pail;
Cheeks like the apples in her father's orchard;
Lips—oh, the poppies in the waving corn;
Eyes like the sky above, serene and empty;
Voice like the clatter of her wooden shoon;
And breath—heaven's breeze itself, blown through the
     byre.

KING (*turning suddenly*).

Know that if fate should bind me to a maid,
She will be worthy of a king for servant.

MADHAVYA.

Is she so fair?...Well, answer were but vain.
'Tis not the man but his condition speaks
When he's in love, or pain; and king and peasant
Roar from the toils with undistinguished groans.
Some are a little fiercer than are others.

[*A pause.*

(*Sings:*)

Stilly flow the waters here;
Shallow is the stream;
All the heavens are blue and clear;
The world is like a dream.

Isles of sand the banks between
'Twixt two heavens lie —
Heaven above the mountains seen,
And heaven that drowseth nigh.

In the wave the river-ox
Floats with still content,
Or, stirring slow, the water rocks,
Along the margin sent.

Round the trees beside the pool
    Couch the deer in shade,
At ease within the covert cool,
    By drowsy branches made.

Yonder where the marshy sedge
    Bows its whispering reeds,
Along the stagnant water edge,
    : *The boar securely feeds.*

Aside is flung the hunter's bow,
    Neglected lies the spear.
Doth his heart contentment know ?
    —Nay, 'tis his to fear.

        [*The* KING *turns away his face.*
        A pause ensues during which
        MADHAVYA *watches him.*

MADHAVYA.

Yet, king and cousin, have, thou mercy on us !

KING.

What dost thou need, O ever-railing cousin ?

What does the restful present not afford thee ?

MADHAVYA.

Change, sire, in its own restfulness. (*Yawning :*) We grow

Stiff in the joints here, like a man that lies
For ever on one side.   Yea, give me rest,
But give me also leave to 'scape the cramp
And doze awhile upon the other side.
Verily, cousin, thou perchance art pious
Beyond thy earlier wont, and findest here
A varied converse that my mind untrained
Scents not, nor views not, but for ever circles
The self-same ground.   Come then, O king and cousin,
Ride thou with us, into the woods, away.
Thy time is nigh — nay, it is come already,
When thou art due.

KING.

Nay, cousin, tell me not !
My time is nigh—but is not due already,
And I will break no plighted troth of mine.
Ride thou ahead.   I follow.   At leisure prey
Upon the lives of brute and bird ; but I
Am sated of their slaughter.

MADHAVYA.

What ! of the sport

Of kings and heroes ?

KING.

God's life is in all things.
There is no life but God's in all his worlds.

MADHAVYA.

O mighty bow, thou art unstrung indeed !
Thou whom no youth save only this could wield,
Thou that wouldst bend to only him, but bowed
Gladly thy breast to him as maid to lord !
O flying shaft, O cruel woman-spirit,
Blind to all else if but that he be pleased,
O wingèd captive, will thy heart not break !

KING.

O shaft and bow !...Up, up, heroic heart !
Meet thou thy insatiate foes, of beasts and men,
In glad-made war, and where the ridgèd spears
Surge in the straits of Death, sweep to new shores !—
Yet here no war. Nor break this peace, my cousin !

MADHAVYA.

Whence is this new-come cruel tenderness !
Whence, but from—come, it is full time, my king ;

And in the chase laugh all this folly away !

KING.

I pray your leave to follow mine own will.

Thine own bent meanwhile follow uncontrolled :

But if thou hunt to wile thy slower way,

Hunt thou remote from here.

MADHAVYA.

     Your promise given

To them that rule these groves, O king, is mine ;

Your vengeance is my own. Nor do I think

These mild-eyed saints are helpless should we err,

Nor go unarmed, though weaponless, among us.

Cold is the crystal to its icy core,

Yet heaven's rays piercing through it burn afar.

Ay ! Save us all from saintly indignation !—

And, cousin king, one whisper ere I go :

Avoid thou love ! I have not done it myself,

And yet—to others—I say " Avoid thou love !"

A rustic maid perchance may cast the net

For greater fish than what she wots of.

KING.

      Go not

With such an error busy in thy brain !

I love no rustic maid, nor ever shall.

If love doth come to me, my love shall be

Queen by true right among all noblest women.

God for her making called all lovely things ;

The willing rose flung down her fragrant load,

The unfolded buds gave innocence, the gems

That gleam in caves—a lonely world below

The perilous feet of searching men—their glory,

Erstwhile unknown ; wild honey from high crags

Above still streams brought sweets ; and saints in
heaven

Added the fruits of solemn lives of prayer—

To form the peerless lady of my dream.

MADHAVYA (*laughing*).

See thou this luscious fruit of all the virtues

Drop not o'erripe into the gaping mouth

Of some dull clown here, yawning through his prayers.

Whom have we here ?   [*Enter* MESSENGERS (*right*).

MESSENGERS.

Victory to the king !

KING.

And to you peace !

1ST MESSENGER.

We bear a message, king.

KING.

Speak then. What news?

MADHAVYA.

I'll wager from the queen,

Speeding you home.

1ST MESSENGER.

O King, the royal mother
Bides still within her palace by your town,
And watches ever how the Ganges' stream,
Like to a clock, whose measure is all Time,
Runs slow away—and dreams upon her son.
Thus with all greetings doth she bid us say:
Now is the season nigh at hand, O king,
Recurrent, when for thee her pains she bore,
Who art her joy. Then bids she thee repair,
By annual wont, to grace her festival
Wherein with sacrifice she thanks the Saints
Who gave thee first, and still have given each year.

KING.

Heaven's blessing on her ! Tell her that I come.

2ND MESSENGER.

The feast is nigh, O king; hence, the fourth day.

KING.

Tell her, her son hath not forgot, and comes.

MESSENGERS.

Victory to the king !

KING.

Peace unto you !

[*The* MESSENGERS *go out.*

(*Sighs :*) Ah me ! ah me ! (*To* MADHAVYA :) Ride,
  cousin, then ; and take

The bulk of all our retinue with thee.

'Tis but three marches hence.   The moon's at full.

March through the cool of eve and dewy night,

And get thee hence a half-march ere thou stay.

At dawn I follow.

MADHAVYA.

What, not now, fair cousin ?

KING.

Nay, sir, not now, nor yet at any time,
Save when I will.

MADHAVYA (*turning*).

Oh, if—

KING.

No, Mádhavya,

Stay, stay! Choose other words for me, that tell
Good comradeship and love. I'm a dumb man
To-day, or mumble all awry.

[*They clasp hands.*

My gift—

This to complete; to bid a long farewell—
Leave me a handful of hard riders. Go!

MADHAVYA.

Till morrow's noon!

[MADHAVYA *goes out (left).*

KING.

Till noon! (*Sighing:*) Ah me, ah me!
Twelve hours to dawn, when I must follow him.
Twelve hours, swift gone, and I must rend my heart,
Where love has drawn with dagger's point his line,

Bleeding. in twain.—They fable wrong who feign
Thou choosest from the sugar-brake thine arms
A-drip with honey, barb'st thine arrows with   .
The blooming mango-cone, wing'st them with bees,
That will not leave the sweetness of the shaft.

Thy bow is the strained arc of frowning heaven ;
Thy string the levin-flash that, quivering, blinds ;
Thy barb, of steel ; thy shaft, though winged as storm,
Is heavy weight of lead, and drags me down (*clutching
at his breast*).

Out, out, thou cruel shaft ! Unloose thine arms,
O barbèd pain ! Let me bound free again !
Lo, thou art doubly cruel, that makest me
As fierce as thou.   Would that these pangs of fire
Shot through her happy breast, that smiling vale,
Which blaze now through my heart's invaded land !
Ah, happy bosom, verdant smiling vale,
Thou little reck'st the fierceness of thy foe !
Nay, not one torch, I would not quench all flames,
To singe thy loaded plains and pleasant pastures,
To lap thy frighted brooks in passing through,
To leap thy towered and gated city walls,
And glut themselves upon a people's woe—

Till all that realm were sorrowful as mine:
Who comes this way ?

[A YOUNG PRIEST *enters* (*left*).

YOUNG PRIEST.

Give you good day, great sir !

KING.

And unto you !

YOUNG PRIEST.

The folk are all astir
Up by the monastery yonder, moving
Hástinapur-wards.   You, sir, go with them ?

KING.

Yea, yea, after a little while I go.

YOUNG PRIEST.

Then fare you well ! I go to gather herbs
And fragrant reeds, laid upon the high altar
In sacrifice.   The matron Gautami
Was urgent with me, too, saying " Bring me home
A herb of potency, for one in fever
Among my maids"—Sakuntala by name,
The very breath of father Kanwa's nostrils.

4

KING.

Is she then ill?

YOUNG PRIEST.

Nay, 'tis some maidish pains.
'Tis a strange burden for a prior; yet he
Loves her as though she were his own. Her father,
Great Viswamítra, widowed, left his throne
Of famed Kanúj, its heavy cares and sorrows,
Its load of worldly fret and earthly show,
Long ere he passed the bounds of earth and heaven;
And fled to heavenly thoughts in solitude
By the far banks of dim Godáveri;
There fleeing, gave the fair babe to our father
Here to uprear. He loves her as his child.
Behold, here is she come, with the two maids
That ever sort with her. I must be going.
Give you goode'en, sir. Time is pushing on.

KING.

Peace be with you! [*The* YOUNG PRIEST *goes out.*
         Now, may the heavens be praised!
For none may say I stooped, who woo my queen.
      [*He gazes out (left) watching the path.*

They come, but slow—slow as the feet of Joy.

—Ah, thou pale moon, high iu the Eastern heaveu

Ere closing day, steep thou this night my soul,

Fevered, in thy cool beams! Yet not thy beams,

Calm like the sea silently fluctuating

Through the long eve, can cool the fever here.

Thou fair deception, thou bright-robed mirage,

That mock'st my throat with cups to slake the fires

Ablaze within, and smilest still to hear

My groans redoubled as I quaff thy fraud!

> [*He gazes out (left).*
>
> PRIYAMVADA (*her voice heard from a little distance*).

Sakúntala! Oh! my Sakúntala!

Rest not too long! Here's what thou fain wouldst see.

> [*She enters with* ANASUYA (*left*).

Ah, then, how strange! The king is come before us!

We three came out to sit, sir, in the grove

A little while, until the moon shall rise,

And sing a song perchance, and slow wend home

Before the dews lie white upon the sward—

We two ahead to make the path for her—

For our dear comrade, sir—a little smooth.

ANASUYA.

For our dear comrade bears a grievous load.

KING.

What ails my lovely lady ? Tell me, swift !

ANASUYA.

She suffers sore.   She saith it was the sun.

KING.

She has been reckless as she walked, fond maid,
And left the shade, where happy trees bowed down
To kiss her head—for some fair flower perchance,
That was not worth one pang of that dear frame ?

ANASUYA.

She has been reckless as she walked, fond maid,
Nor kept the shade, where all of us bowed round
To kiss her head, for some fair flower indeed—
That may be worth all pangs which rack the frame.

KING.

And what the name thou givest to that flower ?

PRIYAMVADA.

She has not told us, king.   Haply such flower

No name receives save it by two be found.

Hast thou such blossom seen ?

KING (*passionately*).

Ah, tell me, maiden.

Think'st thou she e'er could—love me ? See, I suffer !

PRIYAMVADA.

Dost thou love her?

KING.

I love her.   Ay!

PRIYAMVADA.

She comes.

Oh, I too suffer.   Lo, thy suffering ends.

[SAKUNTALA *enters* (*left*).

SAKUNTALA.

Ah !

[*She presses her hand to her breast.
The* KING *for a few moments
strives silently to gain self-
mastery.*

KING.

You are unwell, dear maid ?

SAKUNTALA.

Ay, gracious sir,
I am not well ; I suffer—yet it is
A little thing, and, pray you, think not of it.
'Twill soon be o'er.

KING.

Will it be soon ? If 'twill
Be over soon, I shall rejoice for you.
Yet if you think that 'twill be over soon,
It is not that which I—thought it might be,
By happy chance—by happy chance for me.

PRIYAMVADA (*softly to* ANASUYA).

Come, Anasuya !

ANASUYA.

Yea, I come, dear maid.

[PRIYAMVADA *and* ANASUYA *go out
slowly and unperceived* (*centre*),
and, as they go, look back.

SAKUNTALA   (*dreamily after a pause*).

And what might that chance be ?

KING (*drawing near*).

The chance of heaven.

SAKUNTALA (*smiling*).

Nay, be not so solemn !   'Tis but a little pain.

KING.

And over soon ?

SAKUNTALA (*after a pause, nodding*).

Ay, over very soon.

KING.

Ah !

SAKUNTALA (*looking down*).

Life is over soon ; and with it pain.

KING.

Or endeth pain ere transient life, more brief
Even than brevity ?

SAKUNTALA.

> Yea, lord, some pain.

KING.

As thine, perchance ?

SAKUNTALA.

> I said not so, dear lord.

Pain in the finger, in the eye, the head.

KING.

And in the heart ?

SAKUNTALA.

> That were or brief or long

According to the heart where it might lie.

A little pain finds out a little heart,

Like the sea-snail, in which to dwell ; great pain

Roams through a palace like the gorgeous Sun's,

World-wide before the feet of kingly pain,

Or feet of joy, that ruled ere pain had come.

KING.

They rule alternate.

SAKUNTALA.

> Ah, that joy should die !

KING.

She doth not die, dear maid, but being of heaven
At times to heaven doth fly ; and still returns.
Sometimes she flutters nigh, yet will not come
Quite to the heart.   Then pain doth tyrannise,
Feeling his throne is shaken, and his term
Perchance at hand.   So raves pain in my heart.

SAKUNTALA (*softly*).

And so in mine.   Ah, Pain !

KING (*sighing*).

Ah, Joy !

BOTH.

Ah, Love !

[*They gaze deeply into each other's eyes.*

KING.

Light of my life and soul of all my being,
If I do venture now to tell my love,
Wilt thou be merciful and listen to me ?
Thou art my star, the centre of all heavens,
To guide my way, where all but thee is dim

And still the aching feet sink in the sand,
Hot from the day. Thou art the calm of eve,
After the whirl of noon, the insistent sound
Of running streams, heard by the tired ear,
The shade of palms, while falls the silent dew,
And still the near cicála drones his prayer
And peace to all : so art thou peace to me,
And saving thee there is no peace, but storm.
Thou art my day, not of this sullen world
But of a land apart—where hate is not,
Born of a maggot, yet with ultimate wings
That rasp the hills on either side the vale,
Neither is fear, with dagger in her hand,
Nor slander's pallid lips whence droppeth foam,
Nor envy's eyes a-glare, that squinting see
All things awry, nor charity is slain
By mouthing fangs that snarl above her bones—
But thou art day, bright in a space apart,
Mid belting forests, where the sunbeams play,
And in their circuit softly chanteth peace.

[He takes her hand.

I come a suppliant from that outer world

To this green land, smooth sward 'mid sheltering trees,
And finding here thy marbled-builded shrine,
Although I faint, thus daring I press on,
Unto the silent altar, where I worship.

> [*He kisses her hand, and clasps her to him, striving tenderly to turn her face towards his.*

> SAKUNTALA (*struggling*).

Oh, go, my lord! Begone! You frighten me.

> KING (*releasing her and dropping upon one knee*).

Nay, love, thou hast no cause for fear, but I;
Thou in thy loveliness art terrible.
See, I am humble; lo, thou canst not fear.
O cruel queen, O terrible in beauty,
I kneel to thee, beloved, and kiss thy feet.

> [*He clasps her feet, and then her knees.*

> SAKUNTALA (*turning*).

Ah, they are gone, and I must fight alone,
Where all things cry aloud Oh yield! Oh yield!
I pray you call my comrades back to me.

KING.

Why shouldst thou need them, loved one ?   Dost still
  fear ?

> [*He rises, and clasps her to him.*

SAKUNTALA (*turning to him*).

If thou dost love me utterly, dear lord,
As I love thee, ev'n to the outmost ends
Where love attains, I beg thee, call on them.

KING.

Yea, I will call them.—Yet they are afar.
Trust me a little while, O bride, O queen—
For naught can make thee less, but thou alone.

SAKUNTALA.

Then shall I ne'er be less, till my life end.

> [*She clasps him and lifts her face as
> about to kiss him.*

GAUTAMI (*her voice coming from
a little distance*).

Sakúntala ! Sakúntala, my child !
(*Nearer:*) Where is my own ?   Come then, my love-
  bird, come !

KING (*hoarsely*).

Who is it?

SAKUNTALA.

The holy mother of our convent,
Sage and belovèd Gautami!

GAUTAMI (*calling, nearer*).

My own!
Where is my little sick bird that was ill?

[GAUTAMI *enters.*

SAKUNTALA (*passionately kissing the* KING).
Hide, hide! For I must go.   Wait, still!

[SAKUNTALA *approaches* GAUTAMI.
The KING *conceals himself.*

Yea, mother.

GAUTAMI.

What, nigh at hand! Thou little rogue!   But come;
The shades descend.   Thy fever will return

If thou art late abroad.   Come, foolish one !
Up at the convent there are fine to-do's.

> [GAUTAMI *goes out (left), leading*
> SAKUNTALA, *who looks back. The*
> KING *leans against a tree, bury-*
> *ing his face in his arms.*

CURTAIN,

ACT I, Scene iii.

Scene: *the outskirts of a forest, as before.* Time: *dawn to sunrise.*

[*The* King *and* Sakuntala *are*
discovered. They embrace.

King (*after a long silence*).

Sweet wife and queen !

Sakuntala.

Ah, happy wife and queen !

King.

Sweet as the tranquil night with all its stars,

That pace in meditation through the heavens,

Like banded spirits that have found their bliss,

For ever in a calm unknown on earth,

And view our storm afar; yet know in storm

Good that we wot not of, nor still our winds !

Sweet as the coming dawn, that follows night

Out of the eastern sky, through the cool dew,

With maiden feet flushed like the budded rose !

Look, yonder, look, belovèd ! She comes, she comes !

Bird-heralded—oh, all the innocent life

Astir with joy—joy that the dawn returns

And life, that paused, is with the sun renewed !

Sweet as this tide of life that wells and springs,

Still up and on, from deep mysterious fonts .

Below the secret caverns of the hills,

Below the depths of earth, and sea, and sky,

Sweeping the spirit on to hidden end !

Sweet as is tranquil night, sweet as the dawn,

Sweet as this life—thou art more sweet, belovèd.

SAKUNTALA.

How strange all seems ; how strange ! I am not she

Who heard of passion's woes, and hearing sighed,

But she enthroned that raises him who kneels,

That she may listen to his news of realms,

Far, old, and fair—and, oh, could list for ever.

O king, I love ; and, lo, through love am glad.

[*They embrace.*

KING (*after a long pause*).

The dawn is come.

SAKUNTALA (*reclining in his arms*).

Yea, love.

KING.

And ere the sun
Lifts himself free from yonder eastern line
I must arise and swift be gone.

SAKUNTALA (*raising her head*).

Where, love ?

KING.

After my horsemen to the capital,
With speed of boisterous wind.

SAKUNTALA.

Why, love ?   What haste
Has the king need of ?

KING.

To fulfil his word.

5

SAKUNTALA.

If the king needs, may not she share with him
That shareth all, joys, yea, and sorrow, and need?
Oh, do not leave me now!

KING.

         Beloved, beloved!
For but a little while await, love.   Swift
Will I return.

SAKUNTALA.

    We measure time in absence
Not by the minute or the lapsing hour,
But by the steady dropping from the heart
Wounded and lone.

KING.

    Yea, love, the time is long,
Measured by pain, yet not, timed by the sun.
Listen, belovèd! I must ride with speed,
The utmost at command.   Should I prove liar
Ev'n for love's sake?   My word, beloved, is given.
To part is pain, yea, though a moment's space,
Yet I have learnt from life this lesson well—

Pain is the high heart's opportunity:
With lofty brow meet we its roaring onset.

SAKUNTALA (*burying her face in his shoulder*).
Oh, do not leave me now, not leave me now!
What is this promise, king, that makes thee quit
Her side who needs thee most, when most her need?

KING.

When thou hast children, wife—and should I die,
And one, thy son, raise up before thine eyes
The past of love, long vanished from thy world,
Wouldst thou not claim his word, if pledged to thee,
First of all duties, though a maid should weep?
Yea, love, I know thee. Such my mother too,
Who holds the plighted word I must redeem.
I lingered but for thy sweet sake, and hope's.
Thou wouldst not have the past, beloved, undone?
Nay, nay!—My troop is gone. I must away!

SAKUNTALA.

Wilt thou forget me, king?

KING (*passionately*).

Can I forget?

Canst *thou* forget?

SAKUNTALA (*looking down*).

Nay!

KING.

Can I then forget?

SAKUNTALA (*embracing him and gazing into his eyes*).

I could not so believe, true love and kind.

KING.

I can no more forget this night than thou;
But like a seal stamped on recipient clay
It will lie fixed and pictured on my brain
Till time shall break the stamp and scatter it
Back into elemental dust again—
Or fate shall with ordeal of fiery woe
Burn all my soul, so that it fluctuating
Confusedly stir, nor aught impressed retain.

SAKUNTALA.

Say no more, O belovèd!

KING.

> And when I come,

Not as wild hunter of shy woodland things,

But as the king, with trumpets and with gold,

Purple and scarlet, in all a king's array

To claim my bride, the jewel of the world,

Then shall thy father, holy prior Kanwa,

Crown me full king with thee, thou perfect crown,

And place thee here to lighten all my throne.

> *[He lifts her arms round his neck.*

Art thou content?

SAKUNTALA.

> Say no more, O belovèd.

KING.

Take thou this royal signet ring, O queen.

If aught thy need before I come, though soon,

Send thou thy messenger with this, and all

Will yield him way, ev'n to my inmost chamber,

As to a talisman. Bear it thyself,

And none will do thee harm ; yet ride with caution,

For it has power not over beasts but men.

Art thou content?

SAKUNTALA.

Say no more, O my king.
Farewell !

KING.

Fare thee well, O my queen ! (*Kissing her :*) Away !

[*He tears himself away and strides out
swiftly (right).* SAKUNTALA *remains
standing alone, and when he has
gone falls down weeping.*

CURTAIN.

———o———

ACT II, Scene i.

Scene: *outskirts of a forest in the neighbourhood of a monastery, as before.* Time : *morning.*

[Two Pupils *enter (centre)*.

1ST PUPIL.

—More holy and inspiring than of old,
If that were possible !

2ND PUPIL.

Simplicity

Of life can go no further. Heroes of eld
Were surely thus. We are a lesser race,
Feebler of heart, frailer of body ; our needs
Gender and multiply, a ravening horde,
Frighting us back from all great enterprise.
Ah, for heroic strength such as is his ;
Body and mind fit for all arduous toil,

And after combat rest, as peace serene,

Not overthrown ev'n though the fight be lost,

Not over-confident though it be won !

1ST PUPIL.

Such is our prior.   Praise to the heavens that he

Is safe returned !

2ND PUPIL.

       Blest be henceforth the date

Of yestereve in all our calendar,

That gave him back to us !

1ST PUPIL.

       Would he had come,

Both for his own great sake, whom none would spare,

And for the king's, a few suns earlier !

Here there come women.   Let us slowly on.

         [*They go out (right).*
         Enter PRIYAMVADA *and*
         ANASUYA (*left*).

ANASUYA.

Do what I will—suppress it as I may—

There still returns this feeling of unease.

Would that these days of long suspense were flown !

For, till the future comes, nothing can prove
Beyond dispute it leads no evil with it.

PRIYAMVADA.

Nay, sister, nay! These are the torturing thoughts
That follow in the enfeebled body's train.
Out with them, out! Be brave to overthrow
The sickly tyrant's evil ministers!
So, were the future come, still would there leer
Dim faces at us of the days beyond,
In endless vistas down the lane of time,
Life were all fear, the soul were crazed with terror,
Shrinking and swerving among batlike wings
Through starless night, that should go upright, sister,
Through night as day, with bold heart to the end.
The king is true; a nature high and noble,
Hating all falsehood like a poisonous thing,
Involuntarily, as all must hate
The viper's tongue and fangs upraised to strike.

ANASUYA.

Yea, yea, I know, I know. Oh, thou art right:
I will not fear his truth. But—

PRIYAMVADA.

What " but " now ?

ANASUYA.

Is there no fear our holy father Kanwa
Will blame the past, in her and us ?   O father,
Would thou hadst never gone, or swift returned !
Ere these days fell upon us, all unwarned !

PRIYAMVADA.

Still be of cheer !   The king will claim his own ;
Who, if he claim her not, remains his own.
Our prior yet has never blamed the blameless.
—See, where she comes, lost in her fantasy !
O love, O love ! I am content 1 love not.

    [SAKUNTALA *enters (left) in deep abstraction.*
Let us away.   She craves to be alone.

    [PRIYAMVADA *and* ANASUYA *go out
slowly (centre), looking back.*

    SAKUNTALA *(to self murmuring at intervals).*
O husband...here it was ..come to me...love !

    [*She sits down in complete abstraction.
The* SAGE DURVASAS *clad as an
ascetic enters (right) slowly and
painfully, unnoticed by her.*

DURVASAS.

I am a-weary, daughter ; give me rest,
Shelter and food, for I am weak and old,
And labour under toil beyond my years.
Five lustral orbits of the travelling sun
Thus have I strayed the world, steeping my soul
In commune with the Spirit, seen to the eye
Of this our flesh but in the divers forms
That fleet for ever, calling to all moods,
Would man but hear, in songs of heavenly tone....

> [SAKUNTALA *remains wrapped in*
> *abstraction. The ancient Sage*
> *stands silently before her.*

I am a-weary daughter. Give me rest,
Shelter and food. I labour 'neath my years....

> [*She buries her face in*
> *her hands.*

Twice have I asked of thee, daughter of man,
Help and the succour of the duteous young.
Ere thrice, beware !...I speak thee not in wrath,
For wrath, the flame, has drawn the substances

Whereon it feeds, out of my heart for aye.

Yet shalt thou sin not, uncondemned. Beware!

> [*A pause. Enter* PRIYAMVADA *and*
> ANASUYA (*centre*).

PRIYAMVADA.

The sound came hence. And there she sits, and lo!

DURVASAS.

Thrice have I asked of thee, daughter of God...

> [SAKUNTALA *remains motionless.*

Learn thou of pain, that purifies the spirit,

Lessons of self-forgetfulness, fond maid...

Lo! he who placed the ring upon thy finger,

Pledging his troth thereby, shall break that troth,

Forgetful of the love that dims thy soul.

> [SAKUNTALA *rises, holding out her arms,*
> *and moves away* (*right*),
> *still unconscious.*

> SAKUNTALA (*murmuring brokenly*).

This way...hither...I come...beloved...I come.

> [*She goes out.*

PRIYAMVADA.

O sir, what hast thou said !   What hast thou done!
Lo, the poor maid knows not her fault, nor sees
Aught that her eyes do view nor doth perform
Aught that her bodily frame unled pursues.
The spirit is absent, sir.   What hast thou said !

ANASUYA.

Take thou all reverent greetings from our tongues,
Great sir, instead ; all service from our hands.
Here but recline, and one shall tend thy needs,
And one shall flee ev'n on the wings of the wind
To bring thee food and all guest-offerings.
But, oh, unsay—O sir, unsay those words !

PRIYAMVADA.

Have pity on a maid whose heart is full !

DURVASAS.

I may not thus lightly unpray my prayers ;
Ask now, unask ; shuffle requests with heaven ;
But what is prayed is prayed, the word is said.
Yet since the task is done wherein she failed,
And since you bear part of her burden for her,

Then be it yours part of her doom to raise,
Part of the pain to lift, from shoulders that
Would not have sunk beneath the load that galled...
Lo! he who placed the ring upon her finger,
Pledging his troth thereby, shall break that troth,
Forgetful of his love—but till again
He see the ring, with which their love was sealed.

PRIYAMVADA.

Praised be thy name, great sir, that thou hast heard
The lowly prayer of these thy handmaidens!

ANASUYA.

Great is thy bounty!—O Sakuntala,
Guard thou thy ring, as life depended on it!

DURVASAS (*looking after* SAKUNTALA).

See thou to thy distracted sister, maiden.
She feels afar the woes that are to come.
(*To* PRIYAMVADA:) Lend thy support, fair daughter,
to my steps,
And lead me slow to where are food and shelter.

PRIYAMVADA.

Come, holy father.

DURVASAS (*looking after SA-KUNTALA*).

God have mercy on her !

I am thine instrument, O heaven ! (*To* PRIYAMVADA :)
I come.

[*He places his hand heavily on*
PRIYAMVADA'S *shoulder and
goes out with her* (*left*).

ANASUYA.

O my Sakuntala !   Ah me !

[SAKUNTALA *enters* (*right*).

SAKUNTALA.

Ah me !...

Is that thou, Anasúya? (*Pressing her brows* :) I'm
   strangely wrought
Upon to-day.   Strange...strange ! I had a dream,
I think ; yet have not slept.   Oh, it was naught.
I still will put all dreamlike fears away—

Things of the night, and joy is of the day —
What thinks't thou, Anasúya : did true love
Ever—couldst *thou* ever forget thy love ?

ANASUYA.

Such were not love ; for true love surely loves
For ever and ever.

SAKUNTALA.

Yea, yea ! Sweet Anasuya,
Thou too hast loved, (*kissing her* :) I know it, I know it,
For thou dost know love is all constancy.

ANASUYA.

I have not loved—excepting thee.

SAKUNTALA.

(*To self* :) And yet—

Though all my star of love should crack and break,
Crumble to atoms, showering brightly down
The empty vault of heaven's eternal main,
Down, down, beyond the deepest rays of the sun,
Where dimmer lights prevail, out into cold ;
Yet should I know he loved—he loved—he loved.

—Thou art too young to listen to such things.
Shut thine ears, shut thine eyes—and shut thy lips;

[She kisses her lips.

Dost hear, keep shut thy lips.   I must be wary.
Thou art but still a babe, and those pink ears,
And those blue eyes, wide as the opened heavens,
And those red lips agape to see my passion,
Must hear not, see not, breathe not—no, never
A word—dost hear? My lord would not forgive me.
He is a lord that is a very tyrant,
And, oh! my heart is glad to be his slave.

[She kisses her again, and laughs.

Thou'rt but a babe in the world, Anaṣúya.

ANASUYA.

Has love such power?

SAKUNTALA.

Yea, love is lord of all
Lord of all joys, and since naught can resist him
Is lord of sorrows too—and so, beware!
Art thou alone here?

6

ANASUYA.

Yes, for Priyamváda
Leads the strange saint up to our convent doors.
He bade me stay with thee.

SAKUNTALA.

Saint ? What strange saint ?

ANASUYA.

I know not.

SAKUNTALA.

Thou know'st not ! Didst thou see him ?

ANASUYA.

Yea.
He bade me stay with thee—here, and but now.

SAKUNTALA (*pressing her brows*).

I saw no saint, nor heard him bid thee stay.—
I have been strangely wrought upon.

ANASUYA,

Belovèd
Thou art not well. This hidden love doth swell
Within thy maiden soul too turbulently;

But love avowed shall break through to the sun,
And burgeon into flowers, sweet of the soil,
Beautiful to the eye.   Come, love, avow
Thy hidden passion to our holy father.
See here he comes with Priyamvada.   Speak !
He is all-pitiful, sweet.

> [KANWA *enters with* PRIYAMVADA
> (*left*). SAKUNTALA *stands with
> bowed head before him.*

KANWA.

Hail, daughter, hail !

I give thee joy, my child.

> [SAKUNTALA *kneels and kisses his
> hand.*

ANASUYA (*to* PRIYAMVADA).

The sage reposes ?

PRIYAMVADA.

Ay, in Kanwa's cell.

ANASUYA.

She neither saw

Nor heard.

PRIYAMVADA.

Say not a word; for words would set

Fire to new fears in her.

> [KANWA *raises* SAKUNTALA *and embraces*
> *her.   She stands with bowed head.*

KANWA (*scrutinizing her*).

Hast thou no tongue?

SAKUNTALA (*faintly*).

Hail, father!

KANWA.

"Hail!" A frightened dove the hawk

Had struck at on the wing, and smote her feathers,

Scattering them down the sunny summer air,

Who yet had swerved, and sought the leafy shade,

Where to lie still and nurse her wounded bosom,

So might reply, with such a troubled breath.

Who then has smote my dove?   Where was her flight;

Winged in what open spaces of the air,

Beyond the covert of our spreading trees?

Where hast thou flown? and who has smote thee,
  dove?

SAKUNTALA.

O father, thou wast ever pitiful,

Prone to forgive, and prompt to understand,

Not capable of one uncharity,

But having vision to see an innocent heart

Surprised and snared, even in the nets of wrong.

I know not where I am—yet am I bound,

Nor could I rend my limbs from out the cords,

Although I strove—nor do I longer strive,

That am content within the strings to lie,

Though thus my bosom pants, until his hand

Soothe and shall set me free, not thence to fly.

KANWA (*gently*).

And who the fowler, frightened bird ? And where,

Or nigh or far, the hand to set thee free ?

SAKUNTALA (*murmuring, with averted face*).

Far now, but nigh ere long.

KANWA.

How nigh is long ?

SAKUNTALA (*weeping*).

Ask me no more : I cannot speak for tears.

KANWA.

I would not question thee, if so the sooner
Thy love were led up to its prosperous end.

SAKUNTALA.

I would be humbly silent till he comes,
Nor promise aught on his behalf, who knows
What times and seasons are his own, and knows
That the slow seasons are my own no more.
He is exalted; I am very lowly.
He is the king; and I his handmaiden.

KANWA.

Sayst thou, the king—who late was here?

      SAKUNTALA (*bowing her head*).

                               Ay, sir.

KANWA.

Fit mate for royal maid!   So let it be !—
The times and seasons are his own no more
That once is king; nor can he pick and choose
Between his days, when every day a rumour
With frighted face descends the travelling wain
Within his market-place, hurriedly moving

Before the threatening ranks of coming woe.

Sayst thou thy times no longer are thine own ?—

I am resolved. (*To* PRIYAMVADA :) Call Gautami,
  the matron.

(*To* ANASUYA:) And summon thou Sarngárava and
  others

Whom she shall name. Bid them be prompt to take

The road by eve.

PRIYAMVADA.

Yea, father. (*To* ANASUYA :) It·
is well !

ANASUYA.

Ay! Surely he knows all.

[PRIYAMVADA *and* ANASUYA *go out
(left).* SAKUNTALA *has   sunk
upon her knees and holds the
Prior's hand.*

KANWA.

Thou ere to-night

Shalt move towards thy king. There, by his side,

Mayst thou in woman's dignity abide,

That thou hast new put on.　It is not well
Thou shouldst attend a slow conveniency,
Such as the state commands.　But go thou hence,
Escorted titly by our holy train,
Matron and priests.　They shall deliver thee
Into thy husband's hands, true wife and friend,
A comrade in his evil days and glad,
A gift of price—as wisdom is delivered
Into the keeping of a faithful student.

SAKUNTALA.

O father, thou art wise, and I am foolish ;
Yet, father, let me wait his chosen day.
If he were wroth !

KANWA.

　　　　Then were he not the king
That I have known.　I am resolved, belovèd ;
And in my years place thou a full reliance.

　　　　　　　　　[*He raises her.*

For eve prepare, when the hot day descends.

[*Enter* NUNS (*left*).

SAKUNTALA (*to self*).

He bade me come if I had need of him.
My heart hath need of him, and leads my way.

[*The* NUNS *advance towards*
SAKUNTALA, *and bless her.*

1ST NUN.

Hail to thee, queen; be honoured above women !

2ND NUN.

Hail to thee, bride ; be lovely to thy lord !

3RD NUN.

Hail to thee, wife ; be mother to his child !

SAKUNTALA.

O holy women, if ye will, 'tis given.
(*To self* :) The flood is full : I yield me to the stream,
Slowly a-drift into the middle waters.

[*Enter the matron* GAUTAMI
and MONKS (*left*), *with*
PRIYAMVADA *and* ANASUYA.

GAUTAMI.

Eh, to be sure ! The lamb !   Well, to be sure !

KANWA (*to* GAUTAMI).

O sage and tender matron, be it yours
To lead our loved one to the king's abode,
Where she by right may dwell, henceforth for aye.
These will accompany you, and guard your way.
Swiftly perform your charge ; and swift return.

GAUTAMI.

Ay, very gladly.

MONKS.

Hearing, we obey.

GAUTAMI (*embracing* SAKUNTALA).

My lamb, my bird ! All blessings on thy brow !
Ah, think you now ! Why didst thou tell me not ?

KANWA (*to* MONKS).

Thus shall ye say when ye behold the king :
Prince of our race, and chief of all our clans,
Take thou from us this maid, thy wife, thy queen,
Worthy thy love, worthy the imperial throne.

And this we claim, as justice due to her
And due to thee, thine honour and thy fame,
And due to us, the office that we hold.
With her be prosperous ! Long be your reign !

MONKS..

Ay, reverend father, hearing we obey.

KANWA.

And thou, my daughter—honour thou thy lord,
And honouring him thine honour too will grow.
Watch him not narrowly, for petty doubt
Ousts all the larger inmates of the soul.
If he be harsh, be harsh not in return ;
By patience school him that he patient grow.
When fortune smiles, be not puffed-up with pride
Mild to the weak, be courteous unto all.
Thus to thy husband's household wilt thou bring
Love that is mightier than fortune's frown.

SAKUNTALA.

O father, in my heart I store thy words.

KANWA.

This day, O loved one, leav'st thou me. My heart
Fills with the streams of grief, and my voice fails,
Clutching at words, drowned in the flood of woe.
Mine eyes grow dim, and shades surround my soul.
—Thy future bliss shall make amends for all.—

[They embrace.

Bless her, O sun, nor shine upon her way
Too hotly for her feet, and yet dispel
All ominous clouds afar ! Bless her, ye trees,
Spreading fair shades for her through day, through
     night:
Guard her by day from heat with covert thrown
To spreaded covert down her chequered road ;
By night from dew and all ill emanations !
Bless her, O moon, and all ye radiant stars,
That point to heaven beyond our world of trial !......

[He embraces her.

Let us begone ! The day moves on apace,
And much to do.

GAUTAMI.

Ay, let all stir themselves.

[KANWA, GAUTAMI, *and the* MONKS
move slowly off (left). PRIYAMVADA
and ANASUYA *embrace* SAKUNTALA.

SAKUNTALA (*gazing round*).

Farewell, my girlhood's home ! Farewell, my flowers !
And most of all, O Moonlight of the Grove,
Dear jasmine-sister, long farewell to thee !
Take charge of her when I am gone, dear maids.

PRIYAMVADA.

And to whose charge dost thou leave us, belovèd ?

ANASUYA.

The grove will be a desert, thou being gone.

[*The three girls embrace and weep.*

SAKUNTALA.

Ah, what a wretch am I who thus desert
All that I loved till how few days ago !
Yet in good time shall come those that will steep
Your maiden souls in like forgetfulness.
Then, sisters, shall I grow a dream to you,

This place a dream, yourselves become as dreams,
And all things, turned and changed, to shadows grow.

ANASUYA.

Is love so strange ?

SAKUNTALA.

Perchance 'tis all a dream.
—If I should find that he has waked ere I.

PRIYAMVADA (*eagerly*).

Show him the ring. His love will then return.

ANASUYA.

Ay, love, the ring : 'twas that he pledged thee with.
Guard thou the ring ! Its potency is sure.

PRIYAMVADA.

Yet will thy beauty surer magic prove,
For none can look on thee and fail of love.

GAUTAMI (*her voice heard from a little distance*).
Sakúntala ! Sakúntala, my own !

PRIYAMVADA.

Come, love ! They call.

> [*All move forward (left),*
> SAKUNTALA *leading.*

ANASUYA (*to* PRIYAMVADA).

Alack, we two alone !
Yet all were well, if but the saint had spared
His words of doom.

PRIYAMVADA.

Nay, them the ring doth rule.

> [*All go out (left).*

CURTAIN.

ACT II, Scene ii.

SCENE : *a wayside wood-land spot upon the banks of the river Ganges: on the edge of the near bank (at the back of the stage) is seen the top of a ghât or river-stair of stone, of which the steps descend at a little depth into the hidden margin of the stream: a fire of twigs and dry leaves is burning brightly under one of the trees: the further bank is distant and sparsely wooded.* TIME: *evening; the last rays of the setting sun gleam almost horizontally through the trees; followed by the light of the unseen moon from the opposite quarter of the heavens.*

[SAKUNTALA, GAUTAMI, *and* MONKS *are discovered reclining, or busying themselves with the fire and preparations for the evening meal; the two former somewhat apart.*

1ST MONK.

So far 'tis well.

2ND MONK *(yawning)*.

Ay, very well, indeed.
A pleasant road, say I; and fairer camp
Ne'er welcomed weary bones.

3RD MONK *(yawning)*.

How goes the fire?

For I would gladly eat; and fain withdraw
Quick to the land of dreams to-night.   The rest
After our toil makes me already drowse.

4TH MONK *(yawning)*.

I'm drowsy too.

SAKUNTALA *(to* GAUTAMI*).*

And thou, O reverend mother,

Art thou o'er-wearied by this length of road?

7

GAUTAMI.

Not over-wearied, child, yet glad of pause,
And evening's calm and the night's silences.

2ND MONK.

Yon river's beauty urges one to prayers.
God is most merciful, who leads the soul
Through lovely paths that beckon still to heaven.

GAUTAMI (*to* SAKUNTALA).

Ay, ay, belovèd ! Offer thy thanks to Him ;
Pour forth thy praise like water to the Lord !

[SAKUNTALA *descends the river-stair,
where almost hidden from view
she dips her hands in the river
and pours out a libation.*

1ST MONK.

God hath neglected neither heart nor head
Of the dim lives that rose within His worlds.
All things have double aspect. Seek for truth
Amid His ways : the busy brain but learns
What the heart feels, the perfect love of Heaven,

Learn more, and love more : knowledge feedeth love ;
Nor where the fuel faileth glows the fire.

> [SAKUNTALA *ascending*
> *reclines on one of the*
> *steps near the top of*
> *the river-stair.*

GAUTAMI.

Sing, dear bird, sing !

2ND MONK.

Hush ! the maid sings. Hush there !

SAKUNTALA (*sings*).

Oh, lie and listen ! a melodious choir
    Chants from the wooded field ;
Each verdant blade, with heart a-fire,
    Long praise to Heaven doth yield.

Oh, lie and listen ! for the flowers that run
    At riot through the mead,
Sweet songs do raise, ere low the sun
    Beyond the West shall speed !

And hark, belov'd ! the swaying boughs,
    A-stir with changing day,
No whispering wind with song endows,
    But love their voice doth sway.

And 'neath the rhythm of vocal leaves
    Floats up a lowlier song,
From banks where still the river cleaves
    Harmonious way along.

Oh, lie and listen to the tongues of earth
    That sing the tongue divine !
God's Spirit, through their heavenly birth,
    In each heart runs like wine.

Ah, lie and listen ! In the meadow here,
    Beside the flowing stream,
By eve to sing His praises clear !
    Through night 'neath heaven to dream !

1ST MONK (*pointing*).

What's on the flood there ?

2ND MONK (*gazing,.*
    Shadows.

3RD MONK.

The maid sings well.

She hath persuasion in her tones, and sleep

Follows her voice, as willing as a child.

[SAKUNTALA *rises and*

approaches GAUTAMI.

(*Yawning* :) Oh, ho! The moon begins to shine.

4TH MONK.

'Twere well

If supper were as forward.   How is it there?

Our watching scares the pot.

5TH MONK.

'Tis almost ready.

SAKUNTALA (*to* GAUTAMI).

I wonder what our sweet friends now are doing.

—Sweet Priyamváda! Anasúya dear!

Ye should enjoy with me this peaceful scene—

The spreading flood, God's emblem unto men

Of flowing time; the shaken track of the moon,

Where ripples stir, transient as deeds of men,

Scarce to be heard (so God may list his worlds);
And over all, flood, moon, and balmy air,
The felt security of Heaven's high throne.
Often by night have we discoursed of love
Beneath the moon, or watched the lonely stars,
Less passionate, yet if less passioning
Perchance more near to Heaven—for what is passion?

GAUTAMI.

Ask of the sea why it obeys the moon;
Ask of the waves why still they surge to shore;
And ask the wind why it doth range the air;
Ask these—not otherwise the heart knows passion.

SAKUNTALA.

Oh, thou art sage! Not otherwise my soul
Yearns unto him, and rules itself no more.

GAUTAMI.

Ay, ay!

[SAKUNTALA *rises and moves away.*

4TH MONK.

There's some ill influence in the air.
The pot's bewitched.

5TH MONK.

Speak thou no ill. It boils.

[SAKUNTALA *utters a sharp cry.*

3RD MONK.

What ails the maid ?

GAUTAMI.

What is it ?

SAKUNTALA.

My ring, my ring !
Oh, I have dropped it somewhere.   Prithee, search !
My husband gave it me. (*To* MONKS :) I pray you, sirs!
Aid me in search.

[*They approach and begin searching
with her.*

Ah me ! what have I done !
Oh, what a wretch am I, a foolish thing
I should have watched my finger as I moved,
Nor let mine eye to sleep ; or clasped my hand.
'Twas ever too loose, for it was made for him.

3RD MONK.

It is too dark, maid.   Here we scarce can see.

4TH MONK.

Leave it till dawn. The search is hopeless now,
Ev'n if the loss was here.

3RD MONK.

When was't last seen ?

GAUTAMI.

Ay, love, when didst thou see it last ? Give thought.

SAKUNTALA.

Oh, mother, but I know not. I went apart
That I might kiss his ring — we spoke of love —
And found it gone, and cried aloud to you,
And know no more.

4TH MONK.

'Tis lost upon the road.

5TH MONK (*seated*).

Supper is spoiling fast, here, with delay.

SAKUNTALA (*wringing her hands*).

Oh, pray you, search with me. This glance or that
May light on it and save a world of woe.
It may be near ; just at our feet

3RD MONK.

More like

Upon the road. Search with the sun at morn.

4TH MONK.

Or in the stream below, sunk in the ooze,
Among the river-weeds that knot and fold
Continuous screens before the baffled eye.
Search with the dawn.

SAKUNTALA.

The river—ay, belike!

[*She moves towards the stair.*

GAUTAMI.

Search not to-night, my child : the stream is cold,
And light is none, and with the light is hope.

SAKUNTALA.

I will but glance upon the steps ; no more.

[*She searches. The* MONKS *slowly
return to the fire.*

3RD MONK.

Well, I am hungry.

4TH MONK

Supper spoiling, eh?

5TH MONK (*seated*).

Nay, verily, not if ye sit to it.

Sit down, sit down.

3RD MONK.

Thou'st laboured over-long

That we should fling thy toil rashly away.

I come.

4TH MONK.

And I.   Wait till the light of dawn.

[*The* MONKS *settle down to the meal.*

SAKUNTALA (*returning*).

It is not here. (*To* GAUTAMI :) Oh, I am tired and
sad.   [*She weeps.*

GAUTAMI (*soothing her*).

Eb, what is this? What, tears! Why, what a thing

To see! Ev'n if the ring were truly lost

(And we as yet know not that it is lost,

Until the dawn), loves thy lord it, or thee?

Come, tell me that.   Eh?   It or thee?

SAKUNTALA (*raising her head and
smiling*).

Me, mother.

GAUTAMI.

There! Then what's all this to-do about a ring?
If thou art safe, what more can thy king need?

SAKUNTALA.

It was the ring wherewith he married me.
How will he greet me when he sees it gone?

GAUTAMI.

Pooh! Marriage is when two hearts meet and blend:
The ring has naught to do with married souls.
Tell me no more! I have no patience with thee.

SAKUNTALA.

Do I seem foolish to you, mother?

GAUTAMI.

Ay!
Thou hast been foolish, in thine own sweet way,
Up from a babe. I doubt thou'lt ne'er grow wise.

SAKUNTALA.

Then shall I never grow like thee. For thou
Art very wise, dear mother, sage and strong.

GAUTAMI.

Being very old.

SAKUNTALA.

Nay, thou wast ever wise.

GAUTAMI.

Thinkest thou so?   Ah me!

3RD MONK.

           Cometh content
After a day of toil.

4TH MONK.

Ay!

SAKUNTALA (*to* GAUTAMI, *after a pause*).

           Thou sayest true.

If he shall frown, I'll question him and say
" Lov'st thou thy ring, my lord, or lov'st thou me?
If me, behold me ; if not, let me go."
'Twould never do to hang the head and sigh,
And kiss his hands ; for men are arbitrary.
I think I know what then he will reply.
And if he still show traces of vexation,

Why, with a kiss, a very shower of kisses,

I'll turn him like a springtime scene to smiles

—Nay, one kiss only, till he smile for more.

For till he smile, as the glad fields respond,

He shall but know the promise of a shower;

And I will be the frozen North to him,

Blustering and gray—though with a change of wind

The clouds would break, and be dissolved in tears.

3RD MONK.

What was it like ? Of diamonds ? or of pearls ?

Hast seen the ring ?

4TH MONK.

Not I.

5TH MONK.

Nor I.

6TH MONK.

Nor I.

[*The* 5TH MONK *whispers.*

Ha, ha ! ha, ha !   That were a tale indeed !

CURTAIN.

ACT III.

SCENE: *a pavilion on the parapets of the fortress-palace at Hastinapur; it is situated at the Northern angle of the fortress, and is octagonal in form, and surrounded by a wide verandah which is partly flooded with the morning sunshine: outside is a platform bordered by a low battlement, and steeped in sunlight: beyond is seen the river Ganges, here of great breadth and winding so as to be visible through the arches and above the battlement on either side.* TIME: *morning, about three hours after sunrise.*

[TWO COURTIERS *enter separately.*

1ST COURTIER.

What, is the court then risen? Are you free?

2ND COURTIER.

Yes, happily; at last.   The king has left
The Judgment Hall.   Appeals, one, two, and three,
Decided like a God !   Ah, what a mind !
And my attendance over for the day.
I'm for the air.   The Hall's a noble dome,
But, phew, the crowd—Oh heavens. the odour, sir !
There's scarce a breeze to-day even up here,
Near our belovèd Ganges ; and below,
Down on the Southern side where lies the Hall,
Stirs not a whiff of air, though every door
Gasps at the sunshine, with its throat half-filled
By sweaty citizens, all agog to see,
Oozily urgent while they gape at nothing.
Phew! give me air.   Ride with me up the stream.

1ST COURTIER.

Yea, willingly.

2ND COURTIER.

Come then.

[*They sturt,*

1ST COURTIER.

> Does the king ride?

2ND COURTIER.

No, he is ailing still.

1ST COURTIER (*stopping*).

> Ah, say you so?

'Tis now some days since first he made complaint.
H'm! This is ill. What ails him, should you say?

2ND COURTIER.

His hand is ever at his brow, ev'n thus.
Some pain, strange and continuous, he says,
Gnaws at him there; and with it a vague sense
Of things amiss, some blot upon the brain.

1ST COURTIER.

Ay?

2ND COURTIER.

> So he says; but for my part I gape,

Like a poor rustic in his peasant awe,
At all the treasures of that splendid mind.
Blot there may be, but I see naught amiss.

Question and answer, premiss, judgment, swift
Tumble upon each other from his brain,
Where, if I listen, I but scratch my poll.
He's now at breakfast; shortly may arrive,
To breathe at rest, above our Ganges here,
Till come the embassies.

1ST COURTIER.

> Oh, splendid king!

Ah, what a life of toil! Who'd wear a crown?

2ND COURTIER.

Not I—at least, not his.   He spoils the mart
For crowns.   Such throne were martyrdom to me.

> [*He moves away.*

Come!--Thank the Lord, though I was born a fool,
I still can ride to flout the face of Death
For this grand youth who overtops us all!

1ST COURTIER.

Stay! here he comes.   Pause till he seat himself.

2ND COURTIER.

Ay! To one side.

8

1ST COURTIER.

Truly, he looks unwell.

[*The* KING *enters, with*
MADHAVYA, *the* PRIEST
SOMARATA *and* AT-
TENDANTS (*left*).

KING.

Here there is air. Our Ganges brings the boon,
Who in all gifts is lavish to this land.
O mother of our folk, blest be thy stream !

[*He sits, and gazes long*
at the river.

MADHAVYA.

It is a noble river ; ay, a fair sight !

KING (*after a pause*).

What was I saying ? I forget, dear friend.

MADHAVYA.

You praised the stream, sir.

KING.

Ay ? I thought aloud.

1ST COURTIER (*in a low voice*).

He looks unwell ; nor is his mind at ease.

         [*The* TWO COURTIERS *go out 'right*).
         A PAGE *preludes on the lute.*

KING.

Hush !

         PAGE (*sings, to the lute*).

Lovely is youth, but quickly is it flown.
As some sweet air that comes, nor whence is known.
Fair is the noon, but swift the sun doth fade,
And peering shadows steal, and fill the glade.

Yet after eve there dawneth fairer night,
When from the heavens is drawn their veil of light.
Lo, after day are wider visions shown ;
And from the stars God's closer love is known !

Lovely is youth, but quickly is it gone,
A meteor in the sky, that falling shone.
Nor all our worlds suffice to fill one night ;
The sum of lives is but a meteor-flight.

         [*He continues playing after the*
         song concludes.

KING (*after a pause*).

There is in music such a healing grace
As proves it is divine.   Yea, all things come
From heaven at first, though they be long withdrawn
By dim and desert ways ; yet on the shores,
At length regained, that skirt the seas of heaven,
Greeting such voyagers with spreaded sails
From those fair lands, whither we sail not yet,
Men wait and gaze, daring to hope again.
(*To* PAGE :) Ay, play, my lad !   Thus dost thou draw our hearts
Back to their native heaven.   Play on, play on !

> [*The* KING, MADHAVYA, *and the* PRIEST
> SOMARATA *slowly withdraw into
> the verandah (right centre), and
> stand gazing out*; *others follow.
> The music gradually closes. The*
> CHAMBERLAIN *enters* (*right*).

CHAMBERLAIN (*to* ATTENDANT).

Where is the king ? Scant leisure morn or noon,
Or when the evening draws the shades around
Palace and cottage, and the cottager

For lack of light gives over from his toil—
Scant leisure has a king—such king as ours.
Nor slumber now fills up his nights, but speech
Of things beyond the utmost ken of man,
Which though man see not, if he secs amiss,
Error will sway his councils and his deeds.

ATTENDANT.

He's yonder, on the walls.   What needs him now ?

CHAMBERLAIN.

There comes an embassy of priests to plague him,
Out of the North.   Ay, holy men enow ;
From the famed convent where the Málini
Sweeps broadly down below her native hills.

ATTENDANT.

Cometh great Kanwa ?

CHAMBERLAIN.

    Nay, his messengers,
Bringing a matron and a maid, and word
As yet untold.   Doubtless the old appeal
To royal law where law of priests has failed.

But I must stir, unwilling though I am
To scant his rest, and bid him lift again
The world of care that is a monarch's orb.

> [*The* KING, MADHAVYA, *the* PRIEST
> SOMARATA, *and others approach,*
> *returning.*

'Tis a strange sight to see this lad in years
Father a kingdom ; ay, and from its toil
His soul grow to heroic stature, till
He stand above it, and it weep to him,
And breathe its woes, that he may solace them.

ATTENDANT.

Speak, ere he goes.

CHAMBERLAIN.

> Farewell his leisure, then.

> [*He approaches the* KING.

Victory to the king !

KING.

> And peace to thee !

What is thy news ?

CHAMBERLAIN.

           There comes an embassy

Out of the North, from the Himálayan land ;

Of holy men, whose faméd convent stands

Where Málini sweeps through the darkling woods,

That robe the slopes below her native hills.

With them are two, an ancient dame and grave,

And at her side a maid, surpassing fair.

These wait and crave an audience of the king.

KING.

What is their errand ? Brings the dame complaint ?

And against whom ? or does the maid complain ?

CHAMBERLAIN.

They name no errand, sire, but still profess

They bring their message from the holy sage,

Their prior revered, great Kanwa, and await

Till you shall harken.

KING.

           Kanwa, the sage austere !

With honour bid them come, and, Somaráta,

Priest of this house, and guardian of the flame

Where my hearth glows, the emblem of our prayers,
Fitly receive, and lead them to us here.
Pay to great Kanwa's name all reverence.

                [*The* CHAMBERLAIN *and*
                 SOMARATA *go out* (*right*).

What needs the sage of me ? I would fulfil
All that he asks, so it be in my power.
—O Madhavya, my cousin and my friend,
There sweeps along my brain the sense of woe,
Thundering across the champaign of the mind,
Eating the land, like fire along the plain.
Haply doth Heaven with greater punishment
Visit an erring king than lowlier men ;
And when he sins come embassies to him
From the four quarters of the land he loves,
Announcing death and plague, famine and war.
Such troubled thoughts crowd in upon my mind,
And fill me with misgiving.

MADHAVYA.

                 . You are not well ;
Have not been well for days. I watch you grow
Pale as a girl, king. Rest you from your labours.

COURTIER.

To my mind, sire, these monks but come to pay
Tribute of gratitude they owe to you.

MADHAVYA.

Ay, very like 'tis so.—Come thou with me !
I know a fair retreat where we will stay
Hid from the world, till thou art healed again—
Unless thou art ambitious of the grave.

KING (*smiling*).

Dost thou rebuke me, cousin, for ambition ?

MADHAVYA.

For everything, until thou learn to rest.

KING.

What is ambition ?

MADHAVYA.

     'Tis an evil thing ;
In you a greediness for a good name.

KING.

'Tis to desire the e'er receding line
That bounds the lonely view of voyagers.

While the eye sees, there still is aught beyond ;

Till the eye close, the goal is not attained.

Ah, who would strive to gain himself a name,

That knows the world, how small, how far, how frail,

And nothing in it lasting but the soul,

That leaves the shell, where like the jewelled fly's

Its wings were grown, forgotten when it soars !

The praises men receive while still they live

Are like the flowers that perished yesterday

Upon a tomb ; the praises when men die

Pierce not the coffin to the deafened ear,

Resolved in clay, nor to the heavens afar,

Where spirits dwell, but heed not this dim world.

Who would not rather, if the choice were given,

Quit all this toil and moil of busy streets,

The bawling and the throng, the eyes of hate,

The faction and the lust for transient things,

And wend away into the breathing lanes,

Where sun and shadows meet, and the fields call,

And man may contemplate Heaven and his soul,

And know his soul divine, the child of God !

O Mádhavya, Heaven called me to be king,

To clang in arms, to battle for this land,

To lead the folk, and wage a life of toil ;

Yet were I not the king, how glad would I,

Leaving this whirl of war, make peace my quest !

MADHAVYA.

Our duty is where Heaven has called us, sire.

KING.

Ay, spoken true !...Shrink not from any trial !

...Seek not thine ease, but rather to endure

All blows wherewith man's fate doth weld his soul !

> [*The* KING *and* MADHAVYA *slowly
> withdraw into the verandah,
> and pass out (left centre).*

A PRIEST (*following, to* COURTIER).

He speaketh wisely, sir, the youthful king.

Nor be our care to save our single souls,

That were well lost, so more for Heaven were gained.

> [*The* PRIEST, COURTIER, *and
> others follow the* KING (*left
> centre). The* CHAMBERLAIN *and*
> SOMARATA *re-enter with* THREE
> MONKS (*right*).

CHAMBERLAIN.

Pause here a moment, sirs. We will announce
Your advent to the king. Expect an audience,
Here, and at once.

1ST MONK.

We wait, sirs, with your leave.

[*The* CHAMBERLAIN *and* SOMA-
RATA *approuch the* KING
(*left*).

2ND MONK (*to* 3RD MONK).

Bid Gautami be nigh, nor yet be seen,
Until the king receive us and we call.

[*The* 3RD MONK *goes out* (*right*).

1ST MONK.

I am bewildered 'mid the busy throng.
Our leisured ways sort not with palaces.

2ND MONK.

Ay, thou hast reason. Well, I pity him,
The earnest king, amid these idle crowds.

The laughter of the thoughtless fills the ear,
Yet doth not drown the clang of heavy chains.

> [*The 3rd* MONK *returns (right)*.

3RD MONK.

They 're nigh at hand, somewhat withdrawn.

2ND MONK.

> 'Tis well.

> [*They stand and watch.*

CHAMBERLAIN (*to* KING, *who has turned*).

The embassage of Kanwa's holy monks
Is present, sire, and waits your happy leisure.

KING.

'Tis well. I come. And, Mádhavya, dear friend,
Haste to my mother ; say I come to her
Almost at once, after this embassage.

> [MADHAVYA *goes out (left.*)   *The*
>
> KING *advances.*

2ND MONK (*to* 3RD MONK).

Bid them approach ; the time is nigh at hand.

> *The* 3RD MONK *goes out (right).*

1ST AND 2ND MONKS (*advancing*).

Victory to the king !

KING.

                              And with you peace,
Honour and reverence !   Why come ye, sirs ?

1ST MONK.

We come from Kanwa, sire, the holy sage.

KING.

Honour be to his name !

2ND MONK.

                              Be honour paid !

1ST MONK.

We bear a message unto thee from him.

KING.

Then be it said, that words may fruit in deeds.

                              [GAUTAMI *enters with* SAKUNTALA
                                    veiled, and followed by
                                    MONKS (*right*).

SAKUNTALA (*to* GAUTAMI).

Dear mother, is my love so great a king?
Oh, my fond heart is humble and afraid.

> [*All make way. and* SAKUNTALA
> *is left standing with* GAUTAMI
> *before the* KING.

It is my lord, my king!

GAUTAMI.

Hush, love!   They speak.

1ST MONK.

Thus then he bade us speak, before the king:
Prince of our folk, and lord of all our clans,
Take thou from us this maid, thy wife, thy queen;
Worthy the love thou gav'st, worthy thy throne.

> [SAKUNTALA, *letting fall her veil from her
> face, holds out her arms to the* KING.

SAKUNTALA.

I am thy wife, dear lord, and I am come.

> [*The* KING *stands rigid,
> regarding her.*

2ND MONK (*sternly*),

And this we claim, as justice done to her,
And due to thee, thine honour and thy fame,
And due to this, the office that we hold.

MONKS.

With her be prosperous !   Long may ye reign !

KING (*gazing long at* SAKUNTALA).

Surely mine eyes, as they have never dwelt
Upon so fair a maid, have never yet
Gazed on the features of this maid before.

SAKUNTALA.

My lord, my lord !

KING.

       I stand amazèd, sirs.
What is this wondrous message that ye bring ?
This is my wife, ye say ?

2ND MONK,

       Thy wife, sir king.

KING.

Where met, where wedded, and what time made one ?

GAUTAMI.

Wedded in secret, sire, what time with dawn
Thou fledst alone back to thy palace walls.

KING.

Ah, say ye secretly ?   A secret marriage,
And then denied !   Ye closely touch mine honour.

SAKUNTALA.

O my true lord, what ails you that you treat
My love with scoffs ?—You please to mock, my lord:
I would the laugh were o'er. I am too slow,
Too much inclined unto a serious love,
To taste the savour of the jest, my lord.
Please you, when you have done,

KING.

Here is no jest,
Save that ye jest with me, that am the king.
9

SAKUNTALA.

Haply, my lord, you deem I am not modest,
Who come to you, ere your good time arrived.
My father's wish—ay, mine own too (yea, hear
All of my heart), mine own fond wish as well,
Have brought me thus o'er-early here to you.
If there is fault in this, as hap there is,
You have rebuked it heavily, my lord.

2ND MONK.

More heavily than justly, my lord king.

1ST MONK.

O kingly power, that dost intoxicate
E'en noble minds !

KING (*passionately*).

Hark ye ! a word with you !

I, that have striven to set a pattern to
A noble folk, grow hypocrite and liar,
Tyrant intoxicate, and judge unjust !
Truly, sir priests, ye lack persuasion's tones.
Bid holy Kanwa send ambassadors

More skilled than ye to please an honest man !

(*To* SAKUNTALA :) Lady, it grieves me thus to deal
    with you.

Thine eyes are clear—verily, mountain streams

Abrim—nay, nay, let them not overflow !

A mind, so moulded as thy face, might be

Native of heaven.   (*To self:*) If the sage thus should
    choose

Fit bride for me—ay, ay, may be.   'Twere well.

(*To* SAKUNTALA :) These wise ambassadors have haply
    taught

Thy tongue to err.

SAKUNTALA.

> The truth, my lord, is said.

KING (*in a hard voice*).

What sign or token bring you, lady, then

Of these contracted bonds ?

SAKUNTALA.

> So please you, none.

GAUTAMI.

So please you, sire, indeed, there was a ring.

KING (*eagerly*).

Ah, say you so?   And I have one mislaid
I know not where?   Where is thy ring?

1ST MONK.

'Tis lost.

KING (*smiling*).

Oh ay!   And hast thou seen it, sir?

3RD MONK.

Not I.

KING.

And thou?

4TH MONK.

Not I.

5TH MONK (*answering the* KING'S *look*).

Nor I.

6TH MONK.

Nor I, forsooth.

GAUTAMI.

But I have seen it, king ; a band of gold
Set with a jewel where thy cipher blazed.

KING.

Ay, ay, good dame ! Truly my loss is known ;
The jewel famed, far as thy northern home.
What ? Lost once more ! I would ye brought it me.

GAUTAMI (*supporting* SAKUNTALA).

Nay, sweet, my own ! Be not ashamed, my dove !
Shame cannot reach the fortress of the mind
Where the pure spirit dwells ; but raves afar.

KING.

What other token bring ye ?

SAKUNTALA (*to* GAUTAMI).

Tell him, none.

KING.

What other sign ?

GAUTAMI.

The new life, born in her.

[SAKUNTALA *hides her face
in* GAUTAMI'S *arms and
weeps.*

KING.

Then is she verily wife?

GAUTAMI.

Ay, wife indeed.

KING.

Away! away! I make myself unclean,
That look on her even with passing favour,
A thing corrupt, though beautiful she seem.

SAKUNTALA (*to* GAUTAMI).

So fade my visions of an earthly heaven.
Let us begone, mother; lead me away!

1ST MONK.

What then thine answer to the sage, O king?

KING.

Why, even this—I speak a parable
From nature's book: tell him the guileful cuckoo,
Ere to the sky she wings her sportive flight,
Drops eggs where she has mated not, and leaves,

In careless nests, or where the feeble brood,
The labour of her young.

SAKUNTALA (*raising her head*).
Shame on him !   Shame !

2ND MONK.

And, for the maid, dost thou reject her, King ;
Turn her with ignominy from thy doors ?

KING (*to* SOMARATA).

Good Somaráta, thou in this advise.
Lay no more shame on her than maid can bear.
Haply some wandering rogue hath used my name.

SOMARATA.

So please thee, king, this seemeth good to me,
And if to thee, then be it thus ordained ;
And I will trust the maid to custody
Austere and sage, of penitent womanhood,
Where she shall tarry till her child be born,
And then go free—unless the babe may bear
Signs evident of thy kinghood—when rejoice
That truth have proved itself where falsehood seemed.

KING.

So let it be !

MONKS.

Ay, verily, be it so !

SAKUNTALA.

So shall it not be !   Nay, sirs, give me leave !
Ye have o'erloaded me with shame and woe,
Nor have I spoke—these things are strange to me ;
But ye shall not o'erload me too with chains ;
And, lo, I pass, free as my mountain air.
Thou, king, hast lost a greater treasure than
Thy jewelled crown—love that had circled thee
In all thy ways, love that had gone before
To meet thy foes, love that had fought for thee,
And bled, and died, and asked no more but that
It bled for thee.   Great is thy loss, O king.—
So, fare ye well !   I go.

> *[She covers her face with her veil*
> *and goes out (right), followed at a*
> *distance by* GAUTAMI.   *All watch*
> *them in silence.*

KING (*after a pause, clutching at his heart*).

          So! She is gone.

1ST MONK.

Love turns to bitterness apace, my brothers.

2ND MONK.

Ay, love and speed conceiving bring forth woe.

KING (*in a deep voice*).

Almost I could believe.

       [GAUTAMI *returns hastily.*

GAUTAMI (*to* MONKS).

      What! Do ye dream, sirs!
I am an agèd woman. Her steps are swift,
And mine are slow. Follow her, swiftly! Follow!

      [*The* MONKS *leave quickly. The*
      KING *remains meditating, his*
      courtiers watching him.

CURTAIN.

ACT IV, Scene i.

Scene: *a wayside woodland spot upon the banks of the river Ganges, with a flight of river-stairs descending into the stream at the back, as before : the moon is fading in the West above the river, and the further bank, sparsely wooded, is dimly visible ; a boat and nets float upon the stream, and a sound is heard as of a net being hauled in.* Time: *dawn ; the light steals up from the East.*

> [Two Fishermen *are discovered hauling at a net ; the head and shoulders of one are visible as he stands in the water upon the river stair ; the other is on the bank.*

1st fisherman (*in the water*).

Ho, brother, slow ! There's a great snag in here.

2ND FISHERMAN.

Right, brother ; slow.

1ST FISHERMAN.

Halt !—while I get it out.

(*Shivering :*) Ugh !......ugh !

2ND FISHERMAN.

Ay, ay, 'tis bitter cold.

1ST FISHERMAN.

Thine is the warmer job up there. My teeth
Are chattering in my jaws. ... [*He pulls at the snag.*

Out with thee there,
Son of a fiend, got in the frozen hell !
Tear not the net, malicious one. Begone !—
Haul away, brother ! Pull, and warm the blood !
Bah ! I've an ague.

[*He moves upon the steps.*
Ha ! Here's something sharp

Under my foot upon the oozy stair.

2ND FISHERMAN.

A pebble. Pull !

1ST FISHERMAN.

Ay, very like.   Pull, then !

2ND FISHERMAN.

Haul with a will, and get thyself some warmth.

BOTH FISHERMEN (*chanting mono-tonously*).

Haul-oh! heave-oh ! Haul and pull-oh !
Haul and tug-oh ! Heave-oh ! haul-oh !

1ST FISHERMAN (*pausing*).

'Tis a poor catch, I fear ; like this dull trade.
There's little to be said for a fisher's calling,
But that it keeps a poor man honest still
—Mayhap because it freezes out hot manhood.

2ND FISHERMAN.

Ay, till he learn to keep it in a bottle,
And pour it back again, when work is o'er.

1ST FISHERMAN.

Yea, yea ! True words ! The fisher with his bottle
Is as brave man as robber with his sword.

Yet had our father not begot us fishers
I had as lief have took the sword in hand.

2ND FISHERMAN.

Well, it is fate that son should follow father.
One cannot choose one's sire ; and we were harried
Before we were begot.   So then, the bottle !

1ST FISHERMAN.

Yet with the bottle to my mouth I oft
Think of a change of trade.   What ! Were I brave—
Brave with the bottle empty—then, turning robber—

2ND FISHERMAN.

Soft, brother, soft ! Haul this cursed net again.

1ST FISHERMAN.

(*Softly* :) Eh ?   Who is near ?   (*Loudly* :) 'Tis a less
        sloppy trade,
And therefore only praise I robbery.
If fish flew in dry air, or grew on trees,
I would as lief remain an honest man.

2ND FISHERMAN.

Nay, hold thy tongue, and pull.   There's no one by,
To mark thy native honesty, but me.

1ST FISHERMAN.

Foul waste of words then !

2ND FISMERWAN.

Get the day's job done.

[*Thy haul at the net. The* 1ST
FISHERMAN *moves upon the
stairs.*

1ST FISHERMAN.

Heigh, lad ! There's that sharp-pointed thing again
Here under foot, sunk in the river-ooze.

2ND FISHERMAN.

Kick it away into the stream, and pull.

1ST FISHERMAN.

Nay, let us see it. It feels not like a stone :
'Tis over-sharp.

2ND FISHERMAN.

Bah ! Pull !

1ST FISHERMAN (*feeling with his feet*).

Ah, it is gone !

Over the edge, I fear.

[*He stoops.*

2ND FISHERMAN.

Thou art a fool ;
As arrant blockhead as e'er guzzled mud
Out of a fever-marsh with snipe and eels.

1ST FISHERMAN.

Shall I cast out what the Gods send to us ?

2ND FISHERMAN.

Nay, nay ! Pick up all stones that the Gods lay
Beneath thy feet. They'll serve for wiser men
To stone thee with.

[*The* 1ST FISHERMAN *brings*
up the KING'S *ring.*

Well ! what...eh ? Some foul brass
Off an old woman's finger, that was ate
Up by a crocodile ten years ago !

1ST FISHERMAN (*hiding the ring*).

Ay, very like.   [*He comes out of the water.*

2ND FISHERMAN.

Come ! Let me see it.

1ST FISHERMAN.

What !

Some filthy brass off an old beldam's finger,
Spewed by a crocodile !   Art thou a crow,
Lured by a worthless thing if it but gleam ?

2ND FISHERMAN (*approaching*).

I tell thee, let me see it ; otherwise haply—

1ST FISHERMAN.

Why, in thy wisdom thou might'st stone me with it.

2ND FISHERMAN.

Show ! Is it brass ?

1ST FISHERMAN (*opening his hand*).

Ay, haply—to blind eyes.

Ha, ha ! ha, ha !

2ND FISHERMAN.

Why, it is gold and gems.

[*The* 1ST FISHERMAN
continues to laugh.

Truce to thy jests !   This is a windfall, brother.

1ST FISHERMAN.

Better be lucky than be wise.   Ha, ha!

2ND FISHERMAN.

Best to be both.

1ST FISHERMAN.

Like thee ?—Say thou 'rt a fool,
Or share no luck with me.   Say it, like a man.

2ND FISHERMAN.

If I say " Fool," then share and share alike ?

1ST FISHERMAN.

Ay, if thou make it clear thou art the fool.

2ND FISHERMAN.

Well, to another man I scarce could do it ;
Yet, unto thee—'tis done.

1ST FISHERMAN.

Nay, say it clear:
I am a fool.

2ND FISHERMAN.

Thou art—
10

1ST FISHERMAN.

Nay, then thou hast

No share in mine.

2ND FISHERMAN.

Well, I am fool, my brother.

I were a fool indeed not to say so
For half a fortune.   Show it.   Ah ! ah ! ah !
'Tis a king's seal, belike.

1ST FISHERMAN (*jeering*).

Thy crocodile

Hath ate a king and vomited his crown,
Here at our feet, may be.   Search, brother, search !
Into the water with thee ! (*Laughing loudly*).

2ND FISHERMAN.

Nay thou.   Thou fishest

Best with thy toes ; which, like thine understanding,
Grip in the dirt and clutch up ancient toys.

1ST FISHERMAN.

Ay, nimble brain and nimble toes ; the two
Go ever together.

2ND FISHERMAN.

Thy heels had need
Be nimble too, when thou wouldst sell thy ring.

1ST FISHERMAN.

What! To find purchasers? Verily to-morrow
I will start city-wards, where the king dwells,
And find a buyer in the nearest street
Where there's a jeweller's stall. Find purchasers?
That were not hard.

2ND FISHERMAN.

Nay, but to 'scape the jail.

1ST FISHERMAN.

'Tis a true word. This is a precious thing
To be in poor man's pocket...Almost thou
Persuad'st me it were simpler to turn robber.

2ND FISHERMAN.

'Twould save the justice and police their souls
—And damn thine own.

1ST FISHERMAN.

'Twere virtuously done.

Yet thou sayst truly.   Warily's our word.

Who hastens blindly falls into a well.

Bide then the time, but seize it when it comes.

In with the nets, lad ! Get the day's job done !

BOTH FISHERMEN (*chanting monotonously*).

Heave-oh ! haul-oh ! Haul and pull-oh !

Haul and tug-oh ! Heave-oh ! haul-oh !

[*They continue working.*

CURTAIN.

ACT IV, Scene ii.

SCENE : *an orchard within the outer walls of the palace fortress at Hastinapur : in the foreground (left) is a small pavilion : the orchard reaches down to the river Ganges, the wide expanse of which is seen in the background, and the further side stretching beyond.* TIME: *early evening ; the last gleams of the sun are followed by the light of the full moon among the trees.*

[CHAMBERLAIN *and* SERVANTS
enter (right).

. CHAMBERLAIN.

Quickly to work ! Light ye the lamps here ! Swiftly !

[*The* SERVANTS *light lamps
inside and outside the
pavilion.*

Call thou the singing-boy whose song the king
Commended yester-eve. Perchance his spirit
Will find its solace yet again in music.

> [*A* SERVANT *goes out. An-*
> *other* SERVANT *has entered*
> (*right*).

(*To* SERVANT:) Well, well ! Thine errand ?

SERVANT.

I am bidden to crave
Your urgent presence in the palace, sir.

CHAMBERLAIN.

By whom ?

SERVANT.

'Tis of a ring that's found, sir.

CHAMBERLAIN.

What !

The king's ? 'Tis found ? (*Moving* :) Come, tell me
as we go.

> [*The* CHAMBERLAIN *and* SERVANT
> *go out* (*right*).

1ST SERVANT.

Would I were sick, thus to be saved from pain.

2ND SERVANT.

Ay ! Such a cure were worth the belly-ache.

3RD SERVANT.

Ha, ha ! ha, ha ! Canst not conceive a pain
Elsewhere than in the belly ?

2ND SERVANT.

Nay, I conceive
Naught. 'Twere against all nature.

3RD SERVANT.

Like thy great paunch
Is thy mind swelled but barren ? Some minds teem
With living thoughts ?

2ND SERVANT.

Nay, thank the Gods, I teem
Neither with thought nor child. Who is the wooer
That has assailed thy pregnant mind ? Why didst
Not ask us to the wedding ? Ha ! ha ! ha !
Oh, sight to see !

3RD SERVANT.

Thou hast no mind to wed,

Who hast but belly, where thy joys and pains

Grunt from the sty, and when they squeal thou
    speakest ;

If mind at all, 'tis as a little child,

Scarcely articulate and stumbling still,

With years before it ere the age of fruit.

Thou canst not sympathise with such as kings,

Who know'st no pain save where thou overload'st

The panniers of the patient ass before thee.

2ND SERVANT.

Good friend of royalty, the ass has heels.

3RD SERVANT.

Thou art well panoplied in front : fear not !

1ST SERVANT.

Hist ! Some one comes. Have done ! All ready ?

3RD SERVANT.

Ay !

1ST SERVANT.

Come !

[*The* SERVANTS *go out (left).*
A MAIDEN *enters (right).*

MAIDEN (*gazing round*).

She should be here. No. (*Calling :*) Madhukárika !
Oh, Madhukárika !...Where hast thou hidden ?
—The faithless girl ! (*Calling :*) Oh, Madhukárika !

2ND MAIDEN (*calling, unseen*).

Oh, Parabhrítika !

1ST MAIDEN.

At last ! (*Calling :*) Here ! here !

[*The* 2ND MAIDEN *enters centre).*

2ND MAIDEN.

Oh, here thou art !

1ST MAIDEN.

Yea, verily. Where else ?
Said I not, by the king's pavilion, ere
The vanquished sun fled the pursuing moon ?

2ND MAIDEN.

I come not late, my sweet, but waited thee
Beside the stream.—Oh, night is lovely here,
And in my heart love breaks with spring to bloom !
Look, where the forefront of the embattled stars
Is dimly seen, scouring the heaven's broad plain,
Battalion swift wheeling behind battalion,
Till night shall call her wearied forces halt,
And the pursuit's at pause ; when through the camp
Of heaven sleep reigns, save where the sentinels tread.
Is eve not lovely ?   Does the spring not stir
Strangely within thy maiden bosom too,
Confusing with its motion blood and brain,
Till the eye reel, the body sink and fail,
And the fond spirit seem relapsed and blent
Into the primal scheme of things again,
Into that Love whereout the worlds arose ?

1ST MAIDEN.

Yea, sweet, the spring, and mostly spring by night,
Turneth to love the hearts of all the young.
For youth is spring's, and is but sojourner
In other seasons ; haply guest beloved,

Yet spring its home-land, set in sapphire seas,
To whose white cliffs, topped by far-rolling downs,
Youth ever turns the mirror in the mind ;
And these revisited fill all the throat
With happy, happy, tears.

2ND MAIDEN (*after a pause*).
                            And oh, to think,
Love, after joy, turns tragedy at times !

1ST MAIDEN.

Why sayst thou so ?   I pray it be no omen.

2ND MAIDEN.

Dost thou not mind the lovely maid that came
Saying I am the king's—Sakúntala
Her name—yet the king thrust aside her love.
I ever thought the king in this to blame.

1ST MAIDEN.

They say she was not true.

2ND MAIDEN.
                            Alack the day !
If she was shameless why then did she flee ?

1ST MAIDEN.

If she was blameless why did she not stay ?

2ND MAIDEN.

Ah, every deed looks double, well or ill,
To jar the eyes or soothe, according to
The colours of the web the mind weaves round.

1ST MAIDEN.

Where did she flee ?

2ND MAIDEN.

         None knows : all track was lost.
The matron and the monks that tended her
Returned alone from seeking, and alone,
With many tears, sought their far Northern home.
If she was true a heavy weight must bow
The conscience of the king.

1ST MAIDEN.

         And he is bowed
And ever melancholy. See, they come !

2ND MAIDEN *(looking out)*.

The king himself and courtiers ! Come along.

[*The two* MAIDENS *go out (centre).
The* KING, MADHAVYA, *and the*
PRIEST SOMARATA, *with* COUR-
TIERS, *enter* (*right*).

COURTIER

So please you, sire, rest here awhile. 'Tis cool,
Where the air floats along the sacred stream
On easy pinion. Spring comes apace this year ;
And eager life stirs in the world again.
The mango blooms before its time, and love
Comes with more multitudinous force of flowers
Even than wont.

KING.

       Thou surely art a lover
Thus to praise spring.

COURTIER

       Lover I was when young ;
Nor do forget them all—the dreams of youth.

MADHAVYA.

Thou art more young than this our king, who walks

Past love's fair temple and not lifts an eye,

Nor climbs its steps, nor enters in to worship ;

Who neighbours love—ay, north, south, east, and
west,

On every side—and opens not a door,

Where love may pass the circuit of the walls,

Amid whose shades his heart declines in cold.

KING.

Dost thou rebuke me, Somaráta, too ?

SOMARATA.

Ay, sir ! 'Tis time thy people saw thine heir.

MADHAVYA.

Prithee, sir priest, let the spring work its will

Upon his mind, nor with unskilful reasons

Confuse the battle that it sets before

His obstinate soul, lest with untrusty ranks

And routed a'ds you stubborn all his war.

Let the spring work : 'twill sap these frowning walls.

KING (*sadly*).

Ah, cousin Madhavya, the frowns are thine,

And times are changed, when thy love groweth cold.

MADHAVYA.

My love, nay, verily, O cousin king !

I spoke in haste and dared rebuke the king.

I trusted in his love—that haply fails.

KING.

Thou hast less confidence in thy king than once,

In days now gone.

MADHAVYA.

Nay, sire.

KING.

Ay ! and the folk—

The signs are many. Trust no more the king !

(*Musing* :) The times are changed.—These are the
  spirit's trials—

Which to encounter, and to shock in arms,

Befits those spirits that would hew their way

Through the long serried ranks of this the world,

To the far fields where haply all war ends,

Life is no evil, though of sorrows full,

But life is trial ; trial, opportunity ;

Which opportunity seized is Heaven—and, lost,

Is but the unweaving of a web, oft wove,

To weave again.   Haply the stars have seen,

Beneath the eternal dome, worlds where man's soul

Fruited less rarely to perfection ; yea,

Shall see again.   Lo! they hold up their lamps

Night after night, while æons on the wing,

Scarce audible, here floating far below,

Troop through the arc of time ; and worlds dissolve

Down to their ultimate sands and swiftly flow

Into new heaps that, when their measured hour

Hath built them up, by measured hour decline......

(*After a pause* :) Forgive me, Madhavya! A sense
     of ill

Gropes through my being, like a film at night

Visiting a dreaming brain, of shape unknown,

Dim seen, and spreading terror as a fire

Shakes out the smoky volumes of its train.

MADHAVYA.

Cousin, you are not well.   Ah, take advice

In this . rest you awhile from the state's cares.

KING.

It is not labour in the cares of state
That irks me, Madhavya.

     [He clasps his forehead.

   (*After a pause, to self*:)　May be, may be!

What if 'twere true! (*To* MADHAVYA:)　Tell me—
 they tell me naught—
What news of her, the hapless maid, that fled,
Nor could be found?　Thou wilt remember her.

MADHAVYA.

Yea, I remember well.　No news, my lord.
Her sage companions search no longer here,
But are withdrawn, wearied of hopeless quest.

KING (*suddenly, to* SOMARATA).

Know'st thou the powers of God?

SOMARATA.

    Nay, no man knoweth.

KING.

Know'st thou the powers of man?
11

SOMARATA.

They are as God's,

Or as the beasts, according to the scale
Whereon he stands.

KING.

Can God or man control

The fluctuant images within the brain ?

SOMARATA.

God's ways we know not, king, save in his laws

That guide the worlds, and are, to each, his fate.

Yet, if a mortal sage can curb the mind,

Present or far, controlling to his will

Its intimate thoughts, shall not the Highest have
    power ?

KING.

Or God or man haply my mind controls.

Yet now is change.   My whole soul stirs in arms.

[*The* CHAMBERLAIN *enters,*
        followed by an Attendant
        (*right*).

CHAMBERLAIN.

Victory to the king !

KING.

And peace with thee !

(*To self*:) Peace that my soul knows not, these many
days.

MADHAVYA (*to* CHAMBERLAIN).

He is distraught.

CHAMBERLAIN (*to* MADHAVYA).

Alas ! I know it well.
Alack the day ! alack this famous realm !
Alack for youthful promise unfulfilled !
(*To* KING :) My gracious lord, I bear you welcome news,
Not of a victory, with loss of men,
But of a loss regained.

KING.

Ay, verily ?

What was the loss, and what the gain, old friend ?

CHAMBERLAIN.

Behold the ring, my lord, your signet lost,
And lately found.

King.

Ah, say you so ?

[*He takes the ring.*

Yes, yes, the same; no counterfeit to foil

A careless eye.   Who gave it thee ? Who found ?

Where found he it ?   Tell me ; for it is strange

What blank oblivion bars my searching mind,

Potent to stay it, though invisible,

Where'er it steps upon the strict confine

That borders round this loss.   I fain would pass it.

[*He puts on the ring.*

Chamberlain.

They brought it me but now : 'tis but just found.

And with it comes a tale of fishermen,

Seized and in bonds. I scarce had time to pry

Into the truth of things, yet this I learned.

Two fishers came with dawn into the town,

And lolled and loitered in deserted ways

Until the shops were open, booths arrayed ;

Then wandered still at gaze, stopping at none

Save where the jewellers and smiths of price

Charily bar their shows of gems and gold ;

And still moved on, till in the hottest noon,

Within a narrow lane, where the slant rays

Gain but a passing hold, buried in shade

A hidden shop was found.   There they passed in.

He held them in slow talk of bargaining,

While others stole abroad and woke the law ;

Then rendered them, and this, unto the law.

There now they lie : one weeps, the other cursing ;

And singly each, and both together still

Tell the same tale, that while they fished they found

Within the stream the ring ; and some there are

Say that it lay a-gleaming on the stones,

Some that 'twas found within a fish's maw.

Miracle or plain fact, 'tis here ; and they

Lie in the jail.

KING.

Whence do these fishers come ?

CHAMBERLAIN.

Midway betwixt this city and the low

Ranges of hills that fringe Himálay's snows,

Upon the Ganges' stream.   I gather, sir,

Yourself did pause a while and rest at eve

Upon this self-same spot, riding at speed
From Kanwa's monastery within the hills.
'Tis in the road direct from there to here.

KING (*rising with a distorted face*).

These are not thieves.   Be they released with speed.
Grant them a recompense, and fit reward.

CHAMBERLAIN (*to Attendant*).

Say, they go free.   Summon them to the palace.

[*The Attendant bows and
goes out (right).*

KING (*after a pause, in a low voice*).

What was she called ?

MADHAVYA (*softly*).

Sakúntala, my lord.

KING.

Sakúntala ! Ay ! Memory calls her name.
(*After a pause :*)   It comes, it comes, a flood upon
the brain,
Buffeting all, with waste of waves behind !

[*He groans and trembles, and sits
down. For a long time he remains
rigid with staring eyes and an
expression of horror. His head
gradually sinks. The rest stand
whispering.*

(*Groaning deeply* :) Ah me !

[*He covers his face with his cloak,
and his body is seen to be con-
vulsed. Sounds from the neigh-
bouring city, cries and snatches
of song, intrude upon the quiet
scene.*

CHAMBERLAIN (*to* MADHAVYA).

Ay, touch his valour ! Breathe as the bugle blows !

MADHAVYA (*to* KING).

Thy trial is come, my king. Make broad thy shoul-
ders !

SOMARATA.

Every day is trial.

MADHAVYA.

Not such as this,

Nor such a king to bear.   Up, warrior spirit ¡
Never a call to arms but thou hast heard ¡

        [*The* KING *remains with his
face covered for a while ; then
gradually lowers the cloak.*

    1ST PAGE'S VOICE (*heard singing, at a
distance in the garden*).

       [*The song is heard indistinct-
ly at first, then clearly.*

*Oh, cup of love, fill'd to o'erflowing,
   Bright is thy wine, and strange thy fume !
Yet will I quaff, though nothing knowing
   What change will life through love assume.*

2ND PAGE'S VOICE.

*Oh, flame of love, so brightly burning,
   Thine altar here shall ever glow,
With spiral smokes that, slowly turning,
   Still mount, the heaven's blue vault below.* . . .

1ST PAGE'S VOICE.

Oh, flowers of love, so sweetly blowing,
With golden cores, 'mid petals red !
I wear your crown of blossoms glowing,
Whose brow she kissed, her breast my bed.

2ND PAGE'S VOICE.

Oh, hymn of love, tell thou my yearning,
Be words of fire and outpoured wine,
With woven buds, by worship earning
Her truth in love, whose word is mine !

BOTH VOICES.

Oh, cup of love, abrim, o'erflowing,
Red is thy glow, and strange thy fume !
Yet thus I quaff, though nothing knowing
What change will life through love assume.

> *[As the singers pass on the song*
> *dies in the distance.*

SOMARATA (*to* MADHAVYA).

Speak, sir, again. Your words have potency.

CHAMBERLAIN.

Nay, let them work. Lo! he at last finds tongue.

> *[After a long pause the KING*
> *rises tremulously.*

KING.

O all ye here that see mine agony,
Know that the Heavens have chosen me to be
Subject to shame. Not knowingly I erred ;
Who loving honour's name—lost love as well.

> *[He opens his arms and*
> *calls loudly.*

Sakúntala ! Sakúntala ! Sakúntala !

Where art thou gone ? Canst thou not hear my
call ?

> *[He stands in silence listening*
> *intently.*

MADHAVYA (*to* COURTIERS).

Leave us alone, my lords. May gracious sleep
Brood o'er your couches ! I attend the king.
Nay, Somaráta, stay you here with us !

> *[The* COURTIERS *and* CHAMBERLAIN
> *bow and go out.*

KING.

Nay, nevermore !　Lost once, and found no more !

MADHAVYA.

I see a better flight of ominous wings,
And hear another sound from their far plumes
Than "nevermore."

KING.

What, cousin !　Thou wert ever
A plague in ease, a mediciner in woe.
Prophesy, man !　Point me the flight of wings
On thy horizon.

MADHAVYA.

Look on thy finger, king.
The lost is found—haply by miracle.
Is not the loser worth the care of Heaven ?

KING.

Oh, thou vile ring, that sat upon her finger
As on a throne, and basely fell therefrom !

—Nay, hapless wretch, be thou my sad companion ;

That wooed with me, unenvying, unenvied,

And won with me, and losing dost alone

Share fates with me and know my intimate woe !

(*To* MADHAVYA :) The race of Púru, that in me doth stand,

Juts like a blasted stump above the plain

To bloom no more. The great, the good, are gone ;

Gone Púru's line ! Oh, noble stock accursed,

Whose stem shall fructify no more in souls,

That may attain the perfect growth of heaven !

SOMARATA.

Nay, sire, thou err'st. The seed hath found its soil,

And Púru's stock shall still spread wide its boughs

To cast a shadow o'er the grateful land.

KING.

O my Sakúntala, thy time of joy,

Thy time of woe, that I should half have borne,

Thou bor'st alone ! What thoughts within thy heart

Turned spears on me to slay—what thoughts now
   turn ?

Or, art thou dead, and now, from heaven know'st
   all ?...

(*After a pause* :) Cousin, there is a turmoil in my brain

That I must calm.   Let others rule until

My peace return.   I search for it, and them.

Haply, sirs, I may find her and my peace,

Sweet company, together ; haply my peace

Broodeth alone.   Be this as Heaven ordain.

Let the queen reign, my mother, in my stead,

That ruled before my lamentable reign.

Bid her take counsel with the wise who curb

With me the realm.   Wherein her womanhood

Not readily can appear, appoint with her

. My fittest deputies.   Farewell ! farewell !

I go to cleanse these blots from out my soul.

Let no one follow me !   Farewell, my land !

Thou canst but happily fail of thy king,

Thus stained and thus accurs'd.

MADHAVYA.

Nay, sire !

SOMARATA.

Nay, sire !

KING.

I am as one that runneth in a dream ;
And still must shun the populous haunts of men,
Until this turmoil in the brain give o'er.

> [*He moves away (centre); then*
> *turns.*

Lend me thy cloak, sir priest.

> [*He changes cloaks.*

MADHAVYA (*passionately*).

Thou shalt not go !
Or, where thou goest, I will accompany thee.

KING (*dreamily*).

Let no one follow me.

SOMARATA (*restraining* MADHAVYA).

Cross him not, sir.
Lay not a finger on his labouring soul :
The metal's strained almost to breaking-point.

> [*The* KING *goes out (centre) into*
> *the starlit night.*

CURTAIN.

ACT V, Scene i.

Scene: *a mountain lawn encircled by trees, within the Himalayas ; beyond the lawn the ground slopes downward into a valley, on the other side of which there are seen, between the trees, ranges of mountains rising continually higher, and in the farthest distance appear the eternal snows.*

Time : *afternoon.*

> [*The* Child Bharata *runs on*
> (*left*).

Bharata (*looking back*).

Come, mother, come !   This way, my little love !

> [Sakuntala, *attired in sombre colours as a widow, enters* (*left*). *She embraces the* Child *who has run back to her.*

A FEMALE ATTENDANT *and*
a NURSE *follow.*

ATTENDANT.

Will you sit here, my lady ?

SAKUNTALA.

Willingly.

[*The* ATTENDANT *casts down*
a rug and cushions from
her arms, and kneels.

BHARATA (*growling*).

I am a bear and come to eat thee up.

[*He falls on the kneeling*
ATTENDANT.

ATTENDANT.

Have done, have done ! or will I shoot thee, bear.

BHARATA.

Nay, I will shoot.   Oh, let me get my arrows !

[SAKUNTALA *sits down and*
clasps the CHILD. *The*
CHILD *runs off* (*right*),
followed by the NURSE.

ATTENDANT.

Why are you thoughtful, madam ?

SAKUNTALA.

Am I thoughtful ?

(*After a pause* :) It is a spot most fit for meditation.
Here doth soft peace descend in sun and shade
Out of blue skies, and all the vale is still.
The darkling pines sway soft their poising boughs,
And the grey oaks still rock their tremulous leaves,
Knowing the wind that soothes them is Heaven's love ;
Bees drone amid our chestnut canopy,
Where butterflies in sunshine slow ascend,
And swiftly fall ; and low the dove coos on
From hidden bough, 'mid green leaves overhead.

ATTENDANT (*after a pause*).

I'd welcome sadness, if it left my womb
Filled with so fair a son.

SAKUNTALA.

Thou sayest well.

Sorrow that so endows is very joy.

12

I am content with fate.   Peace here doth dwell,
Where'er this fierce old mountain lord hath rule ;
Peace linking arms with charity, who serves '
Our lovèd lady of these hills ; and he—
Light of mine eyes, the radiance in the air,
Colour in flowers, the music of the streams,
Breath of my nostrils, life of all my world
(For without him were all things pale and dumb)—
O sweetest joy, for ever near my heart,
Where still he wings, from boyish flights abroad !

> [*The* CHILD *and* NURSE
> *return.*

BHARATA.

Now I have arrows, mother.   Do not fear.
If the bear comes, I'll shoot him dead with these.

> [SAKUNTALA *kisses him. He*
> *lays his head in her lap.*

BHARATA.

Sing, mother.

ATTENDANT.

Ay sing, madam, if you will.

SAKUNTALA (*sings*).

There was a maid, ohé! ohé!
　　Who ne'er had loved before.
Her love she gave, ohé! ohé!
　　Her sorrow was full sore.

Her shieldless breast, ohé! ohé!
　　The steel of anguish tore.
Her heart will bear, ohé! ohé!
　　Deep wounds for evermore.

There was a babe, ohé! ohé!
　　It was the babe she bore.
Her love for him, ohé! ohé!
　　Is sea without a shore.

BHARATA (*kissing her*).

Thou art sad, little love?

SAKUNTALA.

Nay, not sad now.

> [*She kisses the* CHILD, *who rises and flings his arms round her neck.*

CURTAIN.

ACT V, Scene ii.

Scene : *a mountain lawn encircled by trees, as before.*
Time: *afternoon. nearing evening.*

> [Madhavya *and* Officers *are dis-*
> *covered :* Madhavya *stands a little*
> *aloof, gazing out (right).*

1st Officer.

Well, sir, what fortune, ou the trail ?   For mine
Is absolute nothing.

2nd Officer.

                  The ibex is less shy
Than this elusive king.   Great as a hunter
He ever was, but in the part of quarry
Even excels that skill which once he showed
Upon the quarry's track.

1ST OFFICER.

                 Doubtless the love
Of his old craft besteads him amply now ;
For news of where he lies lags ever behind
His latest steps.

2ND OFFICER.

             This trail at least seemed sure,
Though after many false.

MADHAVYA (*approaching*).

               'Tis favouring chance,
Not his design, has baffled us ; and still
Can calculation meet and turn and foil
The intricate footsteps of the scheming brain,
And guide them on to where the toils are spread ;
While chance roams free, swifter than thoughts of men.
(*Softly* :) But get ye hid, sirs ! Soft ! We speak too loud.

         [*He puts his finger on his lips and
            points (right).*

1ST OFFICER.

What ! Is it true ?

2ND OFFICER.

Here ?   Is it possible ?

[All look out cautiously.

MADHAVYA.

Yes, he is found.

1ST OFFICER.

And had you speech with him ?

MADHAVYA.

Not yet.   I fear lest the most distant sign
Of this our neighbourhood should scare his feet
From rest again.   Therefore I spied on him,
With still approaches.   He bides here awhile,
All but oblivious of pursuit, and dwells,
Unknown, unquestioned, in yon hermitage.
(*Pointing :*) Their clustering roofs are seen, lo, 'neath
    my hand,
Under the brow of yon impending hill.
But see, he goes ! I'll follow cautiously.

[He goes out (right).

1ST OFFICER (*to* 2ND OFFICER).

Cautiously, sir! Step not too close upon him!
Listen! Who comes behind?

2ND OFFICER (*looking back*).

Women and children.
Here you can see.   They wind along the road.
Nay, but one child with them; that runs before,
And lags behind, and darts to left and right,
And laughs and leaps and claps his little hands.
Oh, 'tis a lad in ten!   Well shouted, boy!

[*The* CHILD BHARATA *runs on shout-
ing* (*left*).

1ST OFFICER.

Pshaw, sir!   Come on!

2ND OFFICER.

Tarry a moment, pray!

[*The* 1ST OFFICER *goes out* (*right*).

(*To* CHILD:) Give thee goode'en!

BHARATA.

Goodeven to thee, too !

2ND OFFICER.

Spoke like a little man.

BHARATA.

Nay, I am big.

2ND OFFICER.

As big as I ?

BHARATA.

Not yet : I shall be, soon.

2ND OFFICER.

And strong ?

BHARATA.

Yes, strong.   See how I jump, I jump.

> [He leaps about. A NURSE
> enters (left) : the CHILD
> runs up to her.

2ND OFFICER.

Well lept, lad ! Thou art like mine own dear child.
I must speak thee fairer, lad, than that.

BHARATA

Where is he ?

2ND OFFICER.

He's at home.

BHARATA.

Where ?

2ND OFFICER.

Far away.

NURSE (*checking* CHILD).

Nay, child, have done ! Nay, Bhára'a !

BHARATA (*to* NURSE).

Who is he ?

NURSE.

I know not, child.

2ND OFFICER (*laughing*).

I am the king's man, boy.

BHARATA.

What king ?

2ND OFFICER.

One lost and lately found.

BHARATA.

My mother calls me king.

2ND OFFICER.

Ay, thou art king—

King of her heart, I wager.

BHARATA.

Here she comes.

Catch me, nurse ! Catch, catch !

[*He runs off laughing (left)*.

NURSE (*clapping her hands*).

Quick ! I come, I come !

(*To* 2ND OFFICER :) You speak in riddles, sir. What
king is this ?

2ND OFFICER.

What king ? Dushyánta, him whose famous walls
Lie mirrored in the holy Ganges' stream,
Where teem the busy marts of Hástinapur.

NURSE.

Oh ay ! My lady once and yet again
Has spoke of such a king.   Such was his name.

2ND OFFICER.

What does thy lady know of courts, nurse ?

NURSE.

Nay,

I'll not say what she knows not, knowing things
I wot not of, so silent all day long.
E'en to the chief she rarely sayeth word,
Though he is old and sage as are his hills ;
And save the ancient lady of the land,
Whose breast she lies in often, knows no mate.

2ND OFFICER.

'Tis a cold spirit, then ?

NURSE.

Nay, there's the boy !

To him her heart is flames—else, cold as snow
That spreads eternal silence o'er yon range,
Where yet the fires beneath rumble and groan,
And may break forth again.

2ND OFFICER.

Yea, verily.

Well, I must follow up my comrade—ay,

Haste too.   Goode'en to you !

[He hurries out (right).

NURSE.

Goodeven, sir !

[The CHILD BHARATA *enters
(left).* SAKUNTALA *follows. The*
CHILD *runs back to her and
embraces her : they advance
across the scene together
(right).* A FEMALE ATTENDANT
follows.

NURSE

Please you, my lady, that way there be men

—Officers of the king, strange to the land.

They questioned me.

SAKUNTALA.

Officers of the king !

What men are these ? Why come they to our vales ?

NURSE.

I know not ; nor how many more they be.
Here there were two. They questioned me amain.

SAKUNTALA.

Why come they now, across our quiet hills ?—
Well, turn we down the vale, where all is still.
What king was he thou spokest of ?

NURSE.

The king ?
Well then, well there ! The name is flown already.
They said he was one lost and lately found.
What that might mean I know not.

SAKUNTALA (after a pause, dreamily).

Lost and found !

NURSE.

He spoke in riddles, till I questioned him.
Then he named names—they perch within my brain,
But, sure, they see me, and flutter off again.
Ay, ay, it comes ! A king, he said, whose walls
Lie mirrored in the sacred Ganges' stream—

Ay, ay ! the city's name ?　Hástinapur.
Yea, that was it.

SAKUNTALA (*after a pause*).

One lost and lately found !

[*Dogs are heard baying.*

BHARATA (*listening*).

Ho, ho !　I hear my dogs.　(*Calling* :)　Come, Swift !
come, Sure !

> [*He runs off (left).* A HUNTSMAN
> *enters (left), accompanied*
> *by the* CHILD, *and leading*
> *a couple of fierce and power-*
> *ful mountain dogs, with*
> *which the* CHILD *sports.*

HUNTSMAN.

Give you good morning, madam !　Little master
Says he be coming down the valley here
Along with me and the dogs.　'Tis but a step.
Sure, he 'll be safe with me ; so sit you here.
I'll bring him back ere long : we must be home
Before eve close.

SAKUNTALA.

We all will come.

HUNTSMAN.

Right welcome !

[*The* CHILD *plays boister-*
ously with the dogs,
which leap upon him.

BHARATA.

Ho, Swift ! ho, Sure !　Look, mother !　Ho, ho, ho !

SAKUNTALA.

Oh, have a care, sir, lest they harm my son !

HUNTSMAN.

Leave them alone, ma'am.　Sure, the dogs well know
Child of that breed.　Ay, ay ! the finest lad
I e'er clapped eyes on—whom my own shall follow
E'en to the death. when their due time shall come.

[SAKUNTALA *takes the* CHILD'S
hand and quiets him.

SAKUNTALA.

Come, let us start.

BHARATA.

Come, Swift! come, Sure! good dogs!

HUNTSMAN (*to* NURSE).

Ay, and the finest lady e'er I saw!
I gauge the lad part by his noble dam.

[SAKUNTALA *and the* CHILD *with
dogs go out (centre)*.

NURSE (*tittering*).

I 'll tell her that.

HUNTSMAN.

I 'll pay thee a kiss to do so.

NURSE.

Pooh!

[*The* HUNTSMAN *goes out, followed by the*
NURSE, *while the* ATTENDANT *flings
down rug and cushions The* CHILD'S
*happy cries and laughter are still heard.
The* TWO OFFICERS *enter (right): the*
ATTENDANT *watches them curiously,
unseen.*

1ST OFFICER.

What, are they flown?

2ND OFFICER.

Ay ! Whither are they turned ?
—'Tis a shrewd mind, indeed, sir !

1ST OFFICER.

Mădhavya's ?

2ND OFFICER.

Ay, he hath brains, and we're a pair of dullards.
He saw at once that it was surely she.

1ST OFFICER.

Well, as for dullard—I scarce saw the child.
My business was to keep in sight the king,
And this I did, ev'n with a single eye.

2ND OFFICER.

Your single eye sees but the half of things,
The empty path.   Range with the other round
The living woods.

1ST OFFICER.

The Lord forbid ! You mean,
Turn still aside to talk with nursing maids.
13

2ND OFFICER.

Nay, 'twas the child, I do protest.

1ST OFFICER

                       Oh ay !

Yet 't was the maid told you your wealth of news.

2ND OFFICER.

Thus, sir, are clues picked up.

1ST OFFICER.

                   And jewels thus

Stick on a muddy shoe.   Now all your life

Will you tramp through the mire, and every night

Search o'er your boots to see what they have found.

2ND OFFICER.

Sir, one would think, to hear this tone of scorn,

Wit lay in finding naught, by foot or brain !

(*Observing* ATTENDANT :) But who is here ? Verily,
    one of them.

What say you—shall we question her ?

1ST OFFICER.

                     Ay, ay !

2ND OFFICER.

See that we scare her not.

1ST OFFICER.

Pshaw ! Bold as daylight,
I will be bound.   Such women are, I find.
Doubtless with you, now, they know better.

2ND OFFICER.

Pooh!

I scarce spoke of the maid, but of the dame.

1ST OFFICER.

Well, be you diplomat among these women,
Mistress and maids.   I schooled in a man's court.
Come ! Speak her fair.   Show how they like it done.

2ND OFFICER.

Cease, cease ! If you would have me question her.

1ST OFFICER.

I'll make allowance for your company,
Some little awkwardness at being seen.
Doubtless alone—

2ND OFFICER.

Nay, speak yourself; I see
You fain would try—though what reply your features
Will bring on us I can anticipate.

1ST OFFICER.

Unlike to you, I care not. (*To* ATTENDANT :) Prithee,
 maid!
Thy name?

ATTENDANT.

Súvrata, sir.

1ST OFFICER.

            Whom dost thou serve?

ATTENDANT.

Are you the king's man that our nurse did tell of?

1ST OFFICER.

Oh, sir, oh, sir! How hast thou filled all hearts—
Ay, and their tongues already wag on thee!
—Nay, maiden, 'twas my lord here.

ATTENDANT.

            What do ye here?

1ST OFFICER.

Come ! What's thy mistress' name ?

ATTENDANT.

Sakúntala.

2ND OFFICER.

Oh, that is well—though half your speech be folly !
So we catch fish with offal.

1ST OFFICER.

And the boy ?

ATTENDANT.

Bhárata, sir.

1ST OFFICER.

And what his father's name ?

ATTENDANT.

Nay. that she knows who bore him.   Ask not me.
(*Starting :*) Sirs, by your leave.

2ND OFFICER.

Haste her return, fair maid.

Thou shalt have handsome payment for thy pains,
I'll warrant thee.   Tell her a life of joy
Is in her grasp if she'll but stretch her hand.

1ST OFFICER.

Ay, if thou lov'st us, tell her thus, fair maid!

ATTENDANT.

This will I say—for love of her, not thee.

[*She goes out (centre*).

1ST OFFICER.

Mádhavya must be told of this with speed.

2ND OFFICER.

Who goes? And who shall keep in touch with these?

1ST OFFICER.

Oh, keep you touch.　You are in touch already.
(*Starting* :) I'll go.　Yet here himself he comes.

2ND OFFICER (*looking out*).

Ev'n so!

[MADHAVYA *enters* (*right*).

MADHAVYA.

See ye lie close!　Startle him not!　He comes.
This way, sirs!　Well, what news?

1ST OFFICER.

Ay, sir ; 'tis she.

MADHAVYA.

And whither flown ?

2ND OFFICER,

Within yon vale ; at hand ;
And to return.

MADHAVYA.

Here ?

1ST OFFICER.

Ay !

MADHAVYA.

And soon ?

1ST OFFICER.

Ere long.

MADHAVYA.

God grant to her capacity of pardon !
For if she pardon not—

1ST OFFICER.

She'll not be queen ! (*Laughs.*)

MADHAVYA.

With queen or no, I seek him for the realm.
Pray Heaven no second loss turn him anew!

[He looks out.

His mien is calm. Grant that his mind be so!
Hist! lest he see you! See, he stirs. Begone!
Yet go not far, sirs. I shall venture on it.

[The OFFICERS *go out (left).* MADHA-
VYA watches the approaching KING,
*then moves forward (right), but
stops.*

Nay, this way still.—Be his heart soft as mine!
Heaven make me wise to choose the fittest words!

[The KING *enters (right), walking in
deep meditation:* MADHAVYA *silently
watches him. After a pause the*
KING *looks up quietly.*

KING.

Ah, Madhavya! so thou hast come!

MADHAVYA.

Yea, king!

Cousin, and lord !

KING.

Thou hast pursued me still !

MADHAVYA.

I did not love thee with a passing love.

KING.

Thou hast pursued me still, although forbid,
Upon the wings of undefeated love ?—
Come then ! Forgive me, O my childhood's friend,
That I forbade what friendship still must give,
Forbidden or allowed !

MADHAVYA.

Oh, friend and king !

[*They embrace.*

KING (*after a pause*).

Yea, Madhavya—I read thy searching eye,
That fears to tread too fast, and stepping forward

Draws ever half-way back—yea, I have suffered,

But now am whole; and after pain health follows.

(*Shaking his head* :) Nay, nothing more.   Joy is more
    fugitive.

MADHAVYA.

Thy people cry for thee.   Oh, come to them !

KING.

Sayest thou so ! ......Beloved and lovely land !

> [*He stretches out his arms
> towards the Southern plains.*

—Nay, till I reach the corner of long time

Before mine eyes, whence to take view, I turn not.

'Tis the last quest.

MADHAVYA.

Whate'er the issue prove,

Happy or hapless, sire—and happiness

Lies with the fates alone—return thou soon.

The voice of all thy people cries—O king !

KING.

Hope and dull fear clasp hands within my heart;

As in the sky by night the stars still shine,

Although the clouds spread broad their level floor
Beneath the heavens, whose roof the starlight gilds
All the night long.   When the winds rock the air,
And all the palace builded thick of films
Quakes to its base and hurls its parapets
Steep down in storm, then, lo, the night grows clear
Unto our eyes, that seen above was clear
Still through the storm—so hope and aching fear
Still touch the one the other in my mind.

MADHAVYA.

Hope ever, king.   Thy fate hath led thee far,
Yet in the end shall lead thee safely home.

KING.

I am not one of those who dwell on Fate,
That 'tis the fiat of the Lord on all
For all in all.   Fate is the natural Law—
By which yon cloud moves silent o'er yon hill,
And herds with those his fleecy kin beyond.
Not so my soul, which though it moves along
Old ways long worn moves partly as it wills,
And ever moving strives with other wills,

That jostle in the road where Chance pell-mell
Drives by converging paths all to one end.
The path of man is naught; happiness, ill,
Fortune, misfortune, station high or low,
All circumstance, are naught—but this is all,
The mien with which the soul meets all that comes.
So God doth test for ultimate heaven all lives
In all His worlds. Ay, though in body bound,
Captives in chains unto the victor Chance,
Driving us on the barren mountain road
Builded by Law along these bitter chasms,
Be we in mind proud, and content, and free!
(*After a pause*:) The queen, my mother, rules she
    still the land?

MADHAVYA.

Ay, but is gray with years.

KING (*sighing*).

Ay me, ay me!

MADHAVYA.

She bears the burden of the state with groans.

KING (*after a pause*).

Take thou this message for me to the queen :
After a little while I come again,
To rule my land, when I shall set her free,
Who fain myself were free unto the end,
Yet enter bonds again for love of her,
Love of the land we serve, and love of Heaven,
Whose worship is the service of mankind.
(*Pointing* :) Look ! when yon narrow moon, that brief
   appears
Within the West, hath moved its circle through,
I will return.   Farewell ! My soul cries out
For space that it may wheel uncramped the sword,
In this last fight.   Till then, farewell ! farewell !

> [*He moves away (right): a few
>   notes of a song are heard
>   faintly: he stops.*

—Hark, hark !   Again !   The woman's   song   once
more !

> [SAKUNTALA'S VOICE *is overheard
>   faintly singing in the dis-
>   tance.*

SAKUNTALA (*sings*).

There was a babe, ohé! ohé!
It was the babe she bore.
Her love for him, ohé! ohé!
Is ocean without shore.

KING.

Who sings ?   Doubtless a maiden of the vale.

MADHAVYA.

Oh ay, belike.   It is a tender song.
A turn of wind carries the rest aside.
—Whate'er this moon bring forth—

KING.

Thou hast my word !
Is it so little worth ?

MADHAVYA.

Oh, king ! my king !

[*The* ATTENDANT *enters*
(*centre*).

ATTENDANT.

And who be ye, my masters ?

MADHAVYA.

The king's men.

Why, maiden, dost thou ask?

ATTENDANT.

What, more king's men!

KING.

Why sayst thou "more"?

ATTENDANT.

The hills are full of them.

KING.

Ah, Mádhavya!

MADHAVYA (*passionately*).

Thinkest thou, king, for such a loss as thou
One man hath mourned? Nay, not one man but all.
Thou hast forgiven me that I searched alone;
Forgive thou now thy subjects each and all.
Ay, ay, the hills are full of searching men,
Yea, all a people searches for its king,
And cries to me to bring him to his own.

[*The* CHILD *enters with* HUNTS-
MAN *and dogs* (*centre*).

BHARATA.

Then, wilt thou take me too, for I am strong ?

HUNTSMAN.

Ay, little master.

BHARATA.

And take me some day soon ?

HUNTSMAN.

Ay, soon enough.

BHARATA (*shouting*).

Ho, Swift! Ho, Sure !

[*He fondles the dogs which
fawn on him.*

To-morrow ?

MADHAVYA (*to self*).

It is the boy. She will be nigh at hand.

KING (*gazing fixedly at the* CHILD).

Who is the child ? Such might have been my own,
Who have no child.—The song, again the song !

SAKUNTALA'S VOICE (*overheard singing
at a little distance*).

*There was a king, ohé ! ohé !
Who loved a maid of yore,
He loved her then, ohé ! ohé !
He loves her now no more.*

[*During the song the* CHILD'S *at-
tention is attracted by the sight
of the* KING. *The* ATTENDANT
*meanwhile sedulously tidies his
disordered dress.*

HUNTSMAN (*to self*).

Come, I'll be off, whilst the lad lets me go.

[*He goes off with dcgs (left).*
KING.

Oh, Mádhavya, love wells up from my heart
Into mine eyes at sight of yon fair child !
Strange how this fatherhood springs up in men,
Who, when the world had moved 'mid starry space
Through how few lustres less, were babes themselves !
A few years more, and he shall change to man

14

The little spirit turning to gravity

From childish things, from weakness to the love

Of all things weak, from joy to love of all

That move in joy, from innocence unto

Passionate hope for them whose innocence

Knows no alloy, and ever a fierce desire

To ward the world from them till they be strong

To walk amid its guileful paths alone.

Blest is the man whose coat is soiled with dust

From little feet awearied on the road,

That claim a trusty refuge in his arms

Whence to laugh fearless down upon the world,

With smiles, sweet to the eye, and innocent words,

Sweet in their artlessness to father's ear !

(*To* CHILD :) Come hither, child ! Thy father must
    be happy !

                [*The* CHILD *advances to him.*

Thou dost not fear me ?

            BHARATA.

      Nay.   [*The* KING *draws the* CHILD *to him.*

           KING.

              Tell me, fair child :

What is thy name ?

BHARATA.

Bhárata.   What is thine ?

KING.

Dushyánta is my name, dear child.

BHARATA.

Art thou

The king's man, too ?

KING.

I am the king, my child.

BHARATA.

Art thou the king ! Then take me with thee, king,
To ride with thee midmost through all thy wars.

KING.

Would I had such a son e'er at my side !
What, canst thou ride ?

BHARATA.

Ay ! Try me.   Make a knee :
Thou shall not throw me though thou strive.

KING.

We'll see.

[*He sets him astride on his knee.* SAKUNTALA *enters with* NURSE (*centre*), *and stands unseen by the* KING.

SAKUNTALA (*to self*).

Ay, it is he ! Peace, O my heart, lie still !

KING.

What, so high, and still on !

BHARATA (*shouting*).

Higher, higher !

MADHAVYA (*to self*).

A lovely lady, worthy to be queen !

KING.

What, harder still ?

BHARATA.

Ay, ay !

KING.

Thou art a horseman,
Skilled, sir, indeed, and bold.

[*He sets him down*

BHARATA.

Wilt thou now take me
Into thy wars to ride and fight beside thee ?

KING.

Yea, lad, if thou wilt come.   Yet thou art young.
Wilt thou not wait till thou art riper grown ?

BHARATA.

Nay, nay !   I'm not so young as I may seem.
But wilt thou take my mother, too ?   I stir not
Unless thou take her too.   She is my love.

KING.

Who is thy mother, child ?

BHARATA.

Nay, call me Bhárata !
'Tis worthier of a soldier.

KING.

Bless thee, Bhárata!

BHARATA.

She is Sakúntala.

KING.

Sakúntala

(*After pause :*) Who is thy father?

BHARATA.

Nay, I have no father.

[*The* KING *hides his face.*

What ails thee, king? Lift up thy head! Be brave!

[*He suddenly sees* SAKUNTALA.

See, mother, see! My king weeps, and I love him.
I am his soldier. Come and help my king!
Speak, mother, speak!

SAKUNTALA (*advancing*).

Be of good cheer, O king!

[*The* KING *looks up. They gaze
long into each other's eyes.*

KING (*in a broken voice*).

Is it thou then, Sakuntala?

SAKUNTALA.

Yea, lord.

KING.

Thou seest my tears.

SAKUNTALA.

Weep not !

KING.

I weep the past,

And all the wrongs, O lady, thou hast known.

SAKUNTALA.

Weep not for me ; I am but little worthy.

KING.

O lady, let thy heart incline to me.
Ask ! I have long in grief and solitude
Sought to atone the sorrows of that day.
I weep the past, thy sorrows, and mine own.

SAKUNTALA.

Weep not for me, lord ; I am little worthy.
Yet for thy sorrows, if thou too hast mourned—
Yea, I shed tears.

[*She weeps.*

KING.

(*To self:*) O Love, where art thou flown ?
Poise o'er her brow once more, brood with thy wings
Upon her breast, and warm her heart again !
—These are in part glad tears I shed, O queen,
That this thy son is mine.   The past is gone,
And with it haply gone thy love for aye,
Yet is thy son my son, and this great soul
That looks out from his eyes upon the world
Is thy soul and is my soul to the end.
So am I glad in part, despite of shame.

(*Approaching :*) Yet is my shame such shame as thou
   mightst still
Forgive, didst thou know all, or didst thou know
Such part as I—who know, myself, not all.
Heaven for my sins, haply to save my soul
—For who can pierce the steeps of Heaven's designs ?—
Breathed o'er the gleaming mirror of my brain,
That half grew dim, though half reflected still
The pictures of past time ; till with the hours,
Upon the sullen mists before the mind,
Thy image, tender, lovely as the dawn,

Stealing with smiles all my sad heart away,

Did reappear, in trust—that broke to tears,

Before the rigid folds that barred the brain.

[*He kneels to her.*

See, love, I kneel to thee. O wife, O queen ;

Be queen and wife again ! Forgive me, still !

SAKUNTALA.

Oh, do not kneel ! I pray thee, lord, arise !

KING.

Not till forgiveness lift my load of shame.

[*He clasps her knees.*

SAKUNTALA (*after a pause*).

Thou art forgiven—if thou canst love me still.

[*She raises him.   They em-
brace. After a long pause
she takes his hand.*

Is this the ring once lost and found again ?

And thou hast found it !

KING.

Strangely it befell.

And now I think on it—ay, ay, 'tis strange—

Swift on its finding, back thy image came,

Never to leave—grant me, O God, my prayer !
—Take it, dear love, again.

SAKUNTALA.

         It played me false,
Nor ever shall again.—Poor ring, 'twas I
To blame, that let thee go, not thou—(*kissing him* :)
   nor thou.
Yet stay thou safe with him.

KING (after a pause).

         So, love, the spring
Again doth break to blossom in our lives.
After our solemn nuptials will we go
Back to that happy land, where Kanwa still
Bides in deep thought the advent of his end.
Mid the old scenes we'll wander, woods and stream,
Where first we loved.   His peace shall fold us round.
Then to the world again, where we must reign.

SAKUNTALA.

O Love, O lord of life, protect us still !
Yet, be thou kind, that now hast tried us well !
O Love, O lord of life, protect us still !

Hear thou, O Love, my queen! [*They embrace.*

SAKUNTALA.

Great is my love,
O lord and king; love that shall circle thee
In all thy ways, love that shall go before
To meet thy foes, love that shall fight for thee,
Yea, though I die—I ask no more but that
I die for thee.   Great is my love, O king!

BHARATA.

Is thy hurt healed again, king?

KING.

Ay, my soldier.—
O Mádhavya, behold my queen and son.

MADHAVYA.

Come, lady; thou art welcome to thy land!
Come thou, with blessings, queen; with copious
showers,
Abundant harvests, and rich offerings.

Unto the Heavens from whom all blessings fall !

—Come, boy, be king hereafter to the folk !

A king that reigneth but for others' weal,

Till from thy labour thou have perfect peace !

—Come, king, for after storm the clouds do clear,

And after blossom-fall doth fruit appear !

All go ou t.

CURTAIN.

END.

Indian Press, Allahabad.